CONTENTS

Hello World
Print Your Name
Print Numbers from 1 to 10
Add Two Numbers
Subtract Two Numbers
Multiply Two Numbers
Divide Two Numbers
Find the Remainder of Two Numbers
Check if a Number is Even or Odd
Convert Celsius to Fahrenheit
Convert Fahrenheit to Celsius
Calculate Simple Interest
Calculate Compound Interest
Calculate Area of a Circle
Calculate Area of a Triangle
Calculate Area of a Rectangle
Calculate Area of a Square
Calculate Volume of a Sphere
Calculate Volume of a Cylinder
Calculate Volume of a Cone
Convert Days to Years, Months, and Days
Check Leap Year
Generate Multiplication Table
Check Prime Number
Find Factorial of a Number
Find Fibonacci Series
Reverse a Number
Check Palindrome Number
Count Vowels in a String
Count Consonants in a String
Convert String to Uppercase
Convert String to Lowercase

Count Words in a Sentence

Find Longest Word in a Sentence

Reverse a String

Check Anagram Strings

Find Largest Number in an Array

Find Smallest Number in an Array

Sum of Array Elements

Reverse an Array

Remove Duplicate Elements from an Array

Merge Two Arrays

Split an Array into Chunks

Sort an Array

Search Element in an Array

Implement Bubble Sort

Implement Selection Sort

Implement Insertion Sort

Implement Merge Sort

Implement Quick Sort

Implement Linear Search

Implement Binary Search

Check Armstrong Number

Check Perfect Number

Generate Random Numbers

Shuffle Array Elements

Calculate GCD of Two Numbers

Calculate LCM of Two Numbers

Find Intersection of Two Arrays

Find Union of Two Arrays

Implement Stack (using Array)

Implement Queue (using Array)

Implement Linked List

Implement Binary Search Tree (BST)

Implement Depth First Search (DFS)

Implement Breadth First Search (BFS)

Reverse a Linked List

Detect Loop in a Linked List

Remove Duplicates from a Linked List

Merge Two Sorted Linked Lists

Implement Hash Table (Hash Map)

Implement Set Data Structure

Implement Priority Queue

Validate Email Address

Validate Password Strength

Validate Credit Card Number

Generate Random Password

Convert Decimal to Binary

Convert Binary to Decimal

Convert Decimal to Octal

Convert Decimal to Hexadecimal

Convert Binary to Octal

Convert Binary to Hexadecimal

Convert Octal to Binary

Convert Octal to Decimal

Convert Octal to Hexadecimal

Convert Hexadecimal to Binary

Convert Hexadecimal to Decimal

Convert Hexadecimal to Octal

Implement Caesar Cipher

Implement Vigenère Cipher

Implement ROT13 Cipher

Implement Bubble Sort Animation

Implement Tic-Tac-Toe Game

Implement Snake Game

Implement Memory Matching Game

Implement Blackjack Game

Implement Quiz Game

Implement Weather Application (API Integration)

Implement To-Do List Application

Implement Calendar Application

Implement Chat Application (using WebSockets)

Implement Calculator

Implement Currency Converter

Implement Countdown Timer

Implement Stopwatch

Implement Pomodoro Timer

Implement Music Player

Implement Video Player

Implement Image Slider

Implement File Uploader

Implement Drawing Application

Implement Markdown Editor

Implement Code Editor

Implement CRUD Operations (using Local Storage)

Implement Authentication System

Implement Role-based Access Control

Implement JWT Authentication

Implement Social Media Login (e.g., Google, Facebook)

Implement Blogging Platform

Implement Portfolio Website

Implement E-commerce Website

Implement Drag and Drop Interface

Implement Responsive Image Gallery

Implement Real-time Data Dashboard

Implement Data Visualization (using D3.js or Chart.js)

Implement Interactive Maps (using Leaflet.js)

Implement Photo Editing Tool

Implement Drawing Board

Implement Video Chat Application

Implement Task Scheduler

Implement Expense Tracker

Implement RSS Feed Reader

Implement URL Shortener

Implement QR Code Generator

Implement Barcode Generator

Implement Password Manager

Implement Word Processor

Implement Online Compiler

Implement Markdown Previewer

Implement 3D Graphics (using Three.js)

Implement WebGL Applications

Implement Voice Recognition

Implement Speech Synthesis

Implement Virtual Keyboard

Implement Virtual Assistant

Implement AI Chatbot

Implement Machine Learning Models (using TensorFlow.js)

Implement Browser Extensions

Implement Web Scraping Tool

Implement Email Client

Implement Music Playlist App

Implement Recipe Finder

Implement Expense Sharing App

Implement Weather Forecast Widget

Implement News Aggregator

Implement Cryptocurrency Tracker

Implement Stock Market Tracker

Implement Flight Booking System

Implement Hotel Booking System

Implement Online Banking System
Implement Healthcare Management System
Implement Inventory Management System
Implement Student Management System
Implement Library Management System
Implement Ticket Booking System
Implement Food Delivery App
Implement Ride Sharing App
Implement Fitness Tracker
Implement Job Portal
Implement Dating App
Implement Social Networking Site
Implement Auction System
Implement Online Gaming Platform
Implement Multiplayer Game
Implement Virtual Reality (VR) Experience
Implement Augmented Reality (AR) App
Implement IoT Applications
Implement Smart Home Automation
Implement Robotics Control System
Implement Drone Control System
Implement Gesture Recognition System
Implement Face Recognition System
Implement Emotion Detection System
Implement Voice-Controlled Applications
Implement Geolocation-based Services
Implement Health Monitoring System
Implement Emergency Response System
Implement Environmental Monitoring System
Implement Smart Farming System
Implement Smart City Solutions
Implement Predictive Analytics System

Implement Data Mining Applications

Implement Blockchain Applications

Implement Cybersecurity Tools

Implement Virtual Classroom

Implement Online Exam System

Implement Digital Wallet

Implement Online Insurance System

Implement E-voting System

Hello World

```
console.log("Hello World");
```

Print Your Name

```
console.log("Your Name");
```

Print Numbers from 1 to 10

```
for (let i = 1; i <= 10; i++) {
  console.log(i);
}
```

Add Two Numbers

```
let num1 = 5;
let num2 = 10;
let sum = num1 + num2;
console.log("Sum:", sum);
```

Subtract Two Numbers

```
let num1 = 15;
let num2 = 7;
let difference = num1 - num2;
console.log("Difference:", difference);
```

Multiply Two Numbers

```
let num1 = 3;
let num2 = 4;
let product = num1 * num2;
console.log("Product:", product);
```

Divide Two Numbers

```
let num1 = 20;
let num2 = 5;
let quotient = num1 / num2;
console.log("Quotient:", quotient);
```

Find the Remainder of Two Numbers

```
let num1 = 10;
let num2 = 3;
let remainder = num1 % num2;
console.log("Remainder:", remainder);
```

Check if a Number is Even or Odd

```
function checkEvenOrOdd(number) {
  if (number % 2 === 0) {
    console.log(number + " is even");
  } else {
    console.log(number + " is odd");
  }
}
checkEvenOrOdd(7); // Example usage
```

Convert Celsius to Fahrenheit

```
function celsiusToFahrenheit(celsius) {
  let fahrenheit = (celsius * 9/5) + 32;
  return fahrenheit;
}
let celsiusTemp = 30;
let fahrenheitTemp = celsiusToFahrenheit(celsiusTemp);
console.log(celsiusTemp + "°C = " + fahrenheitTemp + "°F");
```

Convert Fahrenheit to Celsius

```
function fahrenheitToCelsius(fahrenheit) {
  let celsius = (fahrenheit - 32) * 5/9;
  return celsius;
}
let fahrenheitTemp = 86;
let celsiusTemp = fahrenheitToCelsius(fahrenheitTemp);
console.log(fahrenheitTemp + "°F = " + celsiusTemp + "°C");
```

Calculate Simple Interest

```
function calculateSimpleInterest(principal, rate, time) {
  let interest = (principal * rate * time) / 100;
  return interest;
}
let principalAmount = 1000;
let annualInterestRate = 5;
let timeInYears = 2;
let simpleInterest = calculateSimpleInterest(principalAmount, annualInterestRate,
timeInYears);
console.log("Simple Interest:", simpleInterest);
```

Calculate Compound Interest

```
function calculateCompoundInterest(principal, rate, time) {
  let amount = principal * Math.pow(1 + rate / 100, time);
  let compoundInterest = amount - principal;
  return compoundInterest;
}

let principalAmount = 1000;
let annualInterestRate = 5;
let timeInYears = 2;
```

```
let compoundInterest = calculateCompoundInterest(principalAmount,
annualInterestRate, timeInYears);
console.log("Compound Interest:", compoundInterest);
```

Calculate Area of a Circle

```
function calculateAreaOfCircle(radius) {
  let area = Math.PI * Math.pow(radius, 2);
  return area;
}
let circleRadius = 5;
let areaOfCircle = calculateAreaOfCircle(circleRadius);
console.log("Area of Circle:", areaOfCircle);
```

Calculate Area of a Triangle

```
function calculateAreaOfTriangle(base, height) {
  let area = (base * height) / 2;
  return area;
}
let base = 5;
let height = 8;
let areaOfTriangle = calculateAreaOfTriangle(base, height);
console.log("Area of Triangle:", areaOfTriangle);
```

Calculate Area of a Rectangle

```
function calculateAreaOfRectangle(length, width) {
  let area = length * width;
  return area;
}

let length = 10;
let width = 6;
```

```
let areaOfRectangle = calculateAreaOfRectangle(length, width);
console.log("Area of Rectangle:", areaOfRectangle);
```

Calculate Area of a Square

```
function calculateAreaOfSquare(side) {
  let area = side * side;
  return area;
}
let sideLength = 4;
let areaOfSquare = calculateAreaOfSquare(sideLength);
console.log("Area of Square:", areaOfSquare);
```

Calculate Volume of a Sphere

```
function calculateVolumeOfSphere(radius) {
  let volume = (4/3) * Math.PI * Math.pow(radius, 3);
  return volume;
}
let sphereRadius = 3;
let volumeOfSphere = calculateVolumeOfSphere(sphereRadius);
console.log("Volume of Sphere:", volumeOfSphere);
```

Calculate Volume of a Cylinder

```
function calculateVolumeOfCylinder(radius, height) {
  let volume = Math.PI * Math.pow(radius, 2) * height;
  return volume;
}

let cylinderRadius = 4;
let cylinderHeight = 6;
let volumeOfCylinder = calculateVolumeOfCylinder(cylinderRadius, cylinderHeight);
console.log("Volume of Cylinder:", volumeOfCylinder);
```

Calculate Volume of a Cone

```
function calculateVolumeOfCone(radius, height) {
  let volume = (1/3) * Math.PI * Math.pow(radius, 2) * height;
  return volume;
}

let coneRadius = 5;
let coneHeight = 10;
let volumeOfCone = calculateVolumeOfCone(coneRadius, coneHeight);
console.log("Volume of Cone:", volumeOfCone);
```

Convert Days to Years, Months, and Days

```
function convertDaysToYearsMonthsDays(days) {
  let years = Math.floor(days / 365);
  let remainingDays = days % 365;
  let months = Math.floor(remainingDays / 30);
  let daysLeft = remainingDays % 30;

  return { years, months, daysLeft };
}

let totalDays = 500;
let result = convertDaysToYearsMonthsDays(totalDays);
console.log(result);
```

Check Leap Year

```
function isLeapYear(year) {
  return (year % 4 === 0 && year % 100 !== 0) || (year % 400 === 0);
}
```

```
let year = 2024; // Change the year here
if (isLeapYear(year)) {
  console.log(year + " is a leap year");
} else {
  console.log(year + " is not a leap year");
}
```

Generate Multiplication Table

```
function generateMultiplicationTable(num) {
  for (let i = 1; i <= 10; i++) {
    console.log(num + " x " + i + " = " + (num * i));
  }
}

let number = 7; // Change the number here
generateMultiplicationTable(number);
```

Check Prime Number

```
function isPrime(number) {
  if (number <= 1) {
    return false;
  }

  for (let i = 2; i <= Math.sqrt(number); i++) {
    if (number % i === 0) {
      return false;
    }
  }

  return true;
}
```

```
let num = 13; // Change the number here
if (isPrime(num)) {
  console.log(num + " is a prime number");
} else {
  console.log(num + " is not a prime number");
}
```

Find Factorial of a Number

```
function factorial(number) {
  if (number === 0 || number === 1) {
    return 1;
  }
    let result = 1;
  for (let i = 2; i <= number; i++) {
    result *= i;
  }

  return result;
}
let num = 5; // Change the number here
let fact = factorial(num);
console.log("Factorial of " + num + " is: " + fact);
```

Find Fibonacci Series

```
function fibonacciSeries(count) {
  let fibonacci = [0, 1];

  for (let i = 2; i < count; i++) {
    fibonacci[i] = fibonacci[i - 1] + fibonacci[i - 2];
  }
```

```
  return fibonacci;
}
let numberOfTerms = 8; // Change the number of terms here
let series = fibonacciSeries(numberOfTerms);
console.log("Fibonacci Series:", series.join(", "));
```

Reverse a Number

```
function reverseNumber(number) {
  let reversed = parseFloat(number.toString().split('').reverse().join(''));
  return reversed * Math.sign(number);
}
let num = 12345; // Change the number here
let reversedNum = reverseNumber(num);
console.log("Reversed Number:", reversedNum);
```

Check Palindrome Number

```
function isPalindrome(number) {
  let originalNum = number;
  let reversedNum = parseFloat(number.toString().split('').reverse().join(''));
  return originalNum === reversedNum;
}
let num = 121; // Change the number here
if (isPalindrome(num)) {
  console.log(num + " is a palindrome number");
} else {
  console.log(num + " is not a palindrome number");
}
```

Count Vowels in a String

```
function countVowels(str) {
  let count = 0;
  const vowels = "aeiouAEIOU";

  for (let char of str) {
    if (vowels.includes(char)) {
      count++;
    }
  }

  return count;
}

let sentence = "Hello World"; // Change the sentence here
let vowelCount = countVowels(sentence);
console.log("Number of vowels:", vowelCount);
```

Count Consonants in a String

```
function countConsonants(str) {
  let count = 0;
  const vowels = "aeiouAEIOU";

  for (let char of str) {
    if (!vowels.includes(char) && char.match(/[a-zA-Z]/)) {
      count++;
    }
  }

  return count;
}
```

```
let sentence = "Hello World"; // Change the sentence here
let consonantCount = countConsonants(sentence);
console.log("Number of consonants:", consonantCount);
```

Convert String to Uppercase

```
let str = "hello world"; // Change the string here
let uppercaseStr = str.toUpperCase();
console.log("Uppercase:", uppercaseStr);
```

Convert String to Lowercase

```
let str = "HELLO WORLD"; // Change the string here
let lowercaseStr = str.toLowerCase();
console.log("Lowercase:", lowercaseStr);
```

Count Words in a Sentence

```
function countWords(sentence) {
  let words = sentence.split(" ").filter(word => word.trim() !== "");
  return words.length;
}
let sentence = "This is a sample sentence"; // Change the sentence here
let wordCount = countWords(sentence);
console.log("Number of words:", wordCount);
```

Find Longest Word in a Sentence

```
function findLongestWord(sentence) {
  let words = sentence.split(" ").filter(word => word.trim() !== "");
  let longestWord = "";

  for (let word of words) {
    if (word.length > longestWord.length) {
```

```
      longestWord = word;
    }
  }
    return longestWord;
}
let sentence = "This is a sample sentence"; // Change the sentence here
let longestWord = findLongestWord(sentence);
console.log("Longest word:", longestWord);
```

Reverse a String

```
function reverseString(str) {
  let reversedStr = str.split('').reverse().join('');
  return reversedStr;
}
let str = "Hello World"; // Change the string here
let reversedStr = reverseString(str);
console.log("Reversed String:", reversedStr);
```

Check Anagram Strings

```
function isAnagram(str1, str2) {
  if (str1.length !== str2.length) {
    return false;
  }

  let sortedStr1 = str1.toLowerCase().split('').sort().join('');
  let sortedStr2 = str2.toLowerCase().split('').sort().join('');

  return sortedStr1 === sortedStr2;
}

let string1 = "listen"; // Change the strings here
```

```
let string2 = "silent";
if (isAnagram(string1, string2)) {
  console.log(string1 + " and " + string2 + " are anagrams");
} else {
  console.log(string1 + " and " + string2 + " are not anagrams");
}
```

Find Largest Number in an Array

```
function findLargestNumber(arr) {
  return Math.max(...arr);
}

let numbers = [10, 5, 20, 8, 15]; // Change the array here
let largestNumber = findLargestNumber(numbers);
console.log("Largest Number:", largestNumber);
```

Find Smallest Number in an Array

```
function findSmallestNumber(arr) {
  return Math.min(...arr);
}

let numbers = [10, 5, 20, 8, 15]; // Change the array here
let smallestNumber = findSmallestNumber(numbers);
console.log("Smallest Number:", smallestNumber);
```

Sum of Array Elements

```
function sumArrayElements(arr) {
  return arr.reduce((sum, num) => sum + num, 0);
}

let numbers = [10, 5, 20, 8, 15]; // Change the array here
```

```
let sum = sumArrayElements(numbers);
console.log("Sum of Array Elements:", sum);
```

Reverse an Array

```
function reverseArray(arr) {
  return arr.reverse();
}

let array = [10, 5, 20, 8, 15]; // Change the array here
let reversedArray = reverseArray(array);
console.log("Reversed Array:", reversedArray);
```

Remove Duplicate Elements from an Array

```
function removeDuplicates(arr) {
  return [...new Set(arr)];
}
let array = [10, 5, 20, 8, 15, 10, 5]; // Change the array here
let uniqueArray = removeDuplicates(array);
console.log("Array with Duplicates Removed:", uniqueArray);
```

Merge Two Arrays

```
function mergeArrays(arr1, arr2) {
  return [...arr1, ...arr2];
}
let array1 = [10, 5, 20];
let array2 = [8, 15];
let mergedArray = mergeArrays(array1, array2);
console.log("Merged Array:", mergedArray);
```

Split an Array into Chunks

```
function splitArrayIntoChunks(arr, size) {
  let chunks = [];
  for (let i = 0; i < arr.length; i += size) {
    chunks.push(arr.slice(i, i + size));
  }
  return chunks;
}

let array = [1, 2, 3, 4, 5, 6, 7, 8]; // Change the array here
let chunkSize = 3; // Change the chunk size here
let chunkedArray = splitArrayIntoChunks(array, chunkSize);
console.log("Split Array into Chunks:", chunkedArray);
```

Sort an Array

```
function sortArray(arr) {
  return arr.sort((a, b) => a - b);
}
let numbers = [10, 5, 20, 8, 15]; // Change the array here
let sortedArray = sortArray(numbers);
console.log("Sorted Array:", sortedArray);
```

Search Element in an Array

```
function linearSearch(arr, target) {
  for (let i = 0; i < arr.length; i++) {
    if (arr[i] === target) {
      return i; // Return index if found
    }
  }
  return -1; // Return -1 if not found
}
```

```
let array = [10, 5, 20, 8, 15]; // Change the array here
let targetElement = 20; // Change the target element here
let index = linearSearch(array, targetElement);
if (index !== -1) {
  console.log(`Element ${targetElement} found at index ${index}`);
} else {
  console.log(`Element ${targetElement} not found in the array`);
}
```

Implement Bubble Sort

```
function bubbleSort(arr) {
  let len = arr.length;
  for (let i = 0; i < len - 1; i++) {
    for (let j = 0; j < len - 1 - i; j++) {
      if (arr[j] > arr[j + 1]) {
        [arr[j], arr[j + 1]] = [arr[j + 1], arr[j]]; // Swap elements
      }
    }
  }
  return arr;
}

let array = [10, 5, 20, 8, 15]; // Change the array here
let sortedArray = bubbleSort(array);
console.log("Sorted Array using Bubble Sort:", sortedArray);
```

Implement Selection Sort

```
function selectionSort(arr) {
  let len = arr.length;
  for (let i = 0; i < len - 1; i++) {
```

```
    let minIndex = i;
    for (let j = i + 1; j < len; j++) {
      if (arr[j] < arr[minIndex]) {
        minIndex = j;
      }
    }
    if (minIndex !== i) {
      [arr[i], arr[minIndex]] = [arr[minIndex], arr[i]]; // Swap elements
    }
  }
  return arr;
}

let array = [10, 5, 20, 8, 15]; // Change the array here
let sortedArray = selectionSort(array);
console.log("Sorted Array using Selection Sort:", sortedArray);
```

Implement Insertion Sort

```
function insertionSort(arr) {
  let len = arr.length;
  for (let i = 1; i < len; i++) {
    let current = arr[i];
    let j = i - 1;
    while (j >= 0 && arr[j] > current) {
      arr[j + 1] = arr[j];
      j--;
    }
    arr[j + 1] = current;
  }
  return arr;
}
```

```
let array = [10, 5, 20, 8, 15]; // Change the array here
let sortedArray = insertionSort(array);
console.log("Sorted Array using Insertion Sort:", sortedArray);
```

Implement Merge Sort

```
function mergeSort(arr) {
  if (arr.length <= 1) {
    return arr;
  }

  const mid = Math.floor(arr.length / 2);
  const left = mergeSort(arr.slice(0, mid));
  const right = mergeSort(arr.slice(mid));

  return merge(left, right);
}

function merge(left, right) {
  let result = [];
  let leftIndex = 0;
  let rightIndex = 0;

  while (leftIndex < left.length && rightIndex < right.length) {
    if (left[leftIndex] < right[rightIndex]) {
      result.push(left[leftIndex]);
      leftIndex++;
    } else {
      result.push(right[rightIndex]);
      rightIndex++;
    }
```

```
  }

  return result.concat(left.slice(leftIndex), right.slice(rightIndex));
}

let array = [10, 5, 20, 8, 15]; // Change the array here
let sortedArray = mergeSort(array);
console.log("Sorted Array using Merge Sort:", sortedArray);
```

Implement Quick Sort

```
function quickSort(arr) {
  if (arr.length <= 1) {
    return arr;
  }

  const pivot = arr[arr.length - 1];
  const left = [];
  const right = [];

  for (let i = 0; i < arr.length - 1; i++) {
    if (arr[i] < pivot) {
      left.push(arr[i]);
    } else {
      right.push(arr[i]);
    }
  }

  return [...quickSort(left), pivot, ...quickSort(right)];
}

let array = [10, 5, 20, 8, 15]; // Change the array here
```

```
let sortedArray = quickSort(array);
console.log("Sorted Array using Quick Sort:", sortedArray);
```

Implement Binary Search

```
function binarySearch(arr, target) {
  let low = 0;
  let high = arr.length - 1;

  while (low <= high) {
    let mid = Math.floor((low + high) / 2);
    if (arr[mid] === target) {
      return mid; // Return index if target is found
    } else if (arr[mid] < target) {
      low = mid + 1; // Continue search in the right half
    } else {
      high = mid - 1; // Continue search in the left half
    }
  }

  return -1; // Return -1 if target is not found
}

let sortedArray = [5, 8, 10, 15, 20]; // Change the sorted array here
let targetElement = 15; // Change the target element here
let index = binarySearch(sortedArray, targetElement);
if (index !== -1) {
  console.log(`Element ${targetElement} found at index ${index}`);
} else {
  console.log(`Element ${targetElement} not found in the array`);
}
```

Check Armstrong Number

```
function isArmstrongNumber(num) {
  const digits = num.toString().split('');
  const len = digits.length;
  let sum = 0;

  digits.forEach(digit => {
    sum += Math.pow(parseInt(digit), len);
  });

  return sum === num;
}

let number = 153; // Change the number here
if (isArmstrongNumber(number)) {
  console.log(number + " is an Armstrong number");
} else {
  console.log(number + " is not an Armstrong number");
}
```

Check Perfect Number

```
function isPerfectNumber(num) {
  let sum = 0;

  for (let i = 1; i <= num / 2; i++) {
    if (num % i === 0) {
      sum += i;
    }
  }

  return sum === num && num !== 0;
```

```
}

let number = 28; // Change the number here
if (isPerfectNumber(number)) {
  console.log(number + " is a Perfect number");
} else {
  console.log(number + " is not a Perfect number");
}
```

Generate Random Numbers

```
function generateRandomNumbers(min, max, count) {
  let randomNumbers = [];

  for (let i = 0; i < count; i++) {
    let randomNumber = Math.floor(Math.random() * (max - min + 1)) + min;
    randomNumbers.push(randomNumber);
  }

  return randomNumbers;
}

let min = 1;
let max = 100;
let count = 5;
let randomNumbers = generateRandomNumbers(min, max, count);
console.log("Random Numbers:", randomNumbers);
```

Shuffle Array Elements

```
function shuffleArray(arr) {
  let shuffledArray = [...arr];
```

```
  for (let i = shuffledArray.length - 1; i > 0; i--) {
    const j = Math.floor(Math.random() * (i + 1));
    [shuffledArray[i], shuffledArray[j]] = [shuffledArray[j], shuffledArray[i]];
  }

  return shuffledArray;
}

let array = [1, 2, 3, 4, 5]; // Change the array here
let shuffledArray = shuffleArray(array);
console.log("Shuffled Array:", shuffledArray);
```

Calculate GCD of Two Numbers

```
function calculateGCD(a, b) {
  while (b !== 0) {
    let temp = b;
    b = a % b;
    a = temp;
  }
  return a;
}

let num1 = 36;
let num2 = 60;
let gcd = calculateGCD(num1, num2);
console.log("GCD of", num1, "and", num2, "is", gcd);
```

Calculate LCM of Two Numbers

```
function calculateLCM(a, b) {
  return (a * b) / calculateGCD(a, b);
}
```

```
let num1 = 36;
let num2 = 60;
let lcm = calculateLCM(num1, num2);
console.log("LCM of", num1, "and", num2, "is", lcm);
```

Find Intersection of Two Arrays

```
function findIntersection(arr1, arr2) {
  return arr1.filter(value => arr2.includes(value));
}

let array1 = [1, 2, 3, 4];
let array2 = [3, 4, 5, 6];
let intersection = findIntersection(array1, array2);
console.log("Intersection of Arrays:", intersection);
```

Find Union of Two Arrays

```
function findUnion(arr1, arr2) {
  return [...new Set([...arr1, ...arr2])];
}

let array1 = [1, 2, 3, 4];
let array2 = [3, 4, 5, 6];
let union = findUnion(array1, array2);
console.log("Union of Arrays:", union);
```

Implement Stack (using Array)

```
class Stack {
  constructor() {
    this.items = [];
  }
```

```
  push(element) {
    this.items.push(element);
  }

  pop() {
    if (!this.isEmpty()) {
      return this.items.pop();
    }
    return null;
  }

  peek() {
    return this.items[this.items.length - 1];
  }

  isEmpty() {
    return this.items.length === 0;
  }

  size() {
    return this.items.length;
  }

  clear() {
    this.items = [];
  }
}

// Example usage of Stack
let stack = new Stack();
```

```
stack.push(10);
stack.push(20);
stack.push(30);
console.log("Stack size:", stack.size());
console.log("Top element:", stack.peek());
console.log("Popped element:", stack.pop());
console.log("Stack size after pop:", stack.size());
stack.clear();
console.log("Stack size after clear:", stack.size());
```

Implement Queue (using Array)

```
class Queue {
  constructor() {
    this.items = [];
  }

  enqueue(element) {
    this.items.push(element);
  }

  dequeue() {
    if (!this.isEmpty()) {
      return this.items.shift();
    }
    return null;
  }

  front() {
    return this.isEmpty() ? null : this.items[0];
  }
```

```
  isEmpty() {
    return this.items.length === 0;
  }

  size() {
    return this.items.length;
  }

  clear() {
    this.items = [];
  }
}

// Example usage of Queue
let queue = new Queue();
queue.enqueue(10);
queue.enqueue(20);
queue.enqueue(30);
console.log("Queue size:", queue.size());
console.log("Front element:", queue.front());
console.log("Dequeued element:", queue.dequeue());
console.log("Queue size after dequeue:", queue.size());
queue.clear();
console.log("Queue size after clear:", queue.size());
```

Implement Linked List

```
class Node {
  constructor(data) {
    this.data = data;
    this.next = null;
  }
```

```
}
class LinkedList {
  constructor() {
    this.head = null;
  }

  append(data) {
    const newNode = new Node(data);
    if (!this.head) {
      this.head = newNode;
      return;
    }
    let current = this.head;
    while (current.next) {
      current = current.next;
    }
    current.next = newNode;
  }

  display() {
    let current = this.head;
    while (current) {
      console.log(current.data);
      current = current.next;
    }
  }
}

// Example usage of Linked List
let list = new LinkedList();
list.append(10);
```

```
list.append(20);
list.append(30);
list.display();
```

Implement Binary Search Tree (BST)

```
class TreeNode {
  constructor(value) {
    this.value = value;
    this.left = null;
    this.right = null;
  }
}

class BinarySearchTree {
  constructor() {
    this.root = null;
  }

  insert(value) {
    const newNode = new TreeNode(value);
    if (!this.root) {
      this.root = newNode;
      return;
    }
    this.insertNode(this.root, newNode);
  }

  insertNode(node, newNode) {
    if (newNode.value < node.value) {
      if (!node.left) {
        node.left = newNode;
```

```
    } else {
      this.insertNode(node.left, newNode);
    }
   } else {
    if (!node.right) {
      node.right = newNode;
    } else {
      this.insertNode(node.right, newNode);
    }
   }
  }

 inorderTraversal(node) {
   if (!node) return;
   this.inorderTraversal(node.left);
   console.log(node.value);
   this.inorderTraversal(node.right);
 }
}

// Example usage of Binary Search Tree
let bst = new BinarySearchTree();
bst.insert(50);
bst.insert(30);
bst.insert(70);
bst.insert(20);
bst.insert(40);
bst.insert(60);
bst.insert(80);
bst.inorderTraversal(bst.root);
```

Implement Depth First Search (DFS)

```
class Graph {
 constructor() {
  this.adjacencyList = {};
 }

 addVertex(vertex) {
  if (!this.adjacencyList[vertex]) {
   this.adjacencyList[vertex] = [];
  }
 }

 addEdge(vertex1, vertex2) {
  this.adjacencyList[vertex1].push(vertex2);
  this.adjacencyList[vertex2].push(vertex1);
 }

 depthFirstSearch(start) {
  const visited = {};
  this._dfsHelper(start, visited);
 }

 _dfsHelper(vertex, visited) {
  visited[vertex] = true;
  console.log(vertex);
  for (let neighbor of this.adjacencyList[vertex]) {
   if (!visited[neighbor]) {
    this._dfsHelper(neighbor, visited);
   }
  }
```

```
  }
}
// Example usage of Depth First Search
let graph = new Graph();
graph.addVertex('A');
graph.addVertex('B');
graph.addVertex('C');
graph.addVertex('D');
graph.addEdge('A', 'B');
graph.addEdge('A', 'C');
graph.addEdge('B', 'D');
graph.depthFirstSearch('A');
```

Implement Breadth First Search (BFS)

javascript

Copy code

```
class Graph {
  constructor() {
    this.adjacencyList = {};
  }
  addVertex(vertex) {
    if (!this.adjacencyList[vertex]) {
      this.adjacencyList[vertex] = [];
    }
  }
  addEdge(vertex1, vertex2) {
    this.adjacencyList[vertex1].push(vertex2);
    this.adjacencyList[vertex2].push(vertex1);
  }
  breadthFirstSearch(start) {
    const queue = [start];
    const visited = {};
```

```
    visited[start] = true;

    while (queue.length > 0) {
      const currentVertex = queue.shift();
      console.log(currentVertex);

      for (let neighbor of this.adjacencyList[currentVertex]) {
        if (!visited[neighbor]) {
          visited[neighbor] = true;
          queue.push(neighbor);
        }
      }
    }
  }
}

// Example usage of Breadth First Search
let graph = new Graph();
graph.addVertex('A');
graph.addVertex('B');
graph.addVertex('C');
graph.addVertex('D');
graph.addEdge('A', 'B');
graph.addEdge('A', 'C');
graph.addEdge('B', 'D');
graph.breadthFirstSearch('A');
```

Reverse a Linked List

```
class Node {
  constructor(data) {
    this.data = data;
```

```
    this.next = null;
  }
}

function reverseLinkedList(head) {
  let prev = null;
  let current = head;

  while (current) {
    let next = current.next;
    current.next = prev;
    prev = current;
    current = next;
  }

  return prev;
}
// Example usage of Reverse a Linked List
let head = new Node(1);
head.next = new Node(2);
head.next.next = new Node(3);
head.next.next.next = new Node(4);

console.log("Original Linked List:");
let current = head;
while (current) {
  console.log(current.data);
  current = current.next;
}

head = reverseLinkedList(head);
```

```
console.log("Reversed Linked List:");
current = head;
while (current) {
  console.log(current.data);
  current = current.next;
}
```

Detect Loop in a Linked List

```
class Node {
  constructor(data) {
    this.data = data;
    this.next = null;
  }
}

function detectLoop(head) {
  let slow = head;
  let fast = head;

  while (fast && fast.next) {
    slow = slow.next;
    fast = fast.next.next;

    if (slow === fast) {
      return true; // Loop detected
    }
  }

  return false; // No loop found
}
```

```
// Example usage to detect loop in a Linked List
let head = new Node(1);
head.next = new Node(2);
head.next.next = new Node(3);
head.next.next.next = new Node(4);

// Creating a loop for demonstration purpose (connecting last node to second node)
head.next.next.next.next = head.next;

if (detectLoop(head)) {
  console.log("Loop detected in the Linked List");
} else {
  console.log("No loop found in the Linked List");
}
```

Remove Duplicates from a Linked List

```
class Node {
  constructor(data) {
    this.data = data;
    this.next = null;
  }
}

function removeDuplicates(head) {
  let current = head;

  while (current && current.next) {
    if (current.data === current.next.data) {
      current.next = current.next.next; // Skip the duplicate node
    } else {
```

```
      current = current.next; // Move to the next node
    }
  }
  return head;
}

// Example usage to remove duplicates from a Linked List
let head = new Node(1);
head.next = new Node(1);
head.next.next = new Node(2);
head.next.next.next = new Node(3);
head.next.next.next.next = new Node(3);

console.log("Linked List with Duplicates:");
let current = head;
while (current) {
  console.log(current.data);
  current = current.next;
}

head = removeDuplicates(head);

console.log("Linked List after removing Duplicates:");
current = head;
while (current) {
  console.log(current.data);
  current = current.next;
}
```

Merge Two Sorted Linked Lists

```
class Node {
  constructor(data) {
    this.data = data;
    this.next = null;
  }
}

function mergeTwoSortedLists(l1, l2) {
  let dummy = new Node(0);
  let current = dummy;

  while (l1 && l2) {
    if (l1.data <= l2.data) {
      current.next = l1;
      l1 = l1.next;
    } else {
      current.next = l2;
      l2 = l2.next;
    }
    current = current.next;
  }

  current.next = l1 || l2;

  return dummy.next;
}

// Example usage to merge two sorted Linked Lists
let list1 = new Node(1);
list1.next = new Node(3);
```

```
list1.next.next = new Node(5);

let list2 = new Node(2);
list2.next = new Node(4);
list2.next.next = new Node(6);

console.log("First Sorted Linked List:");
let current = list1;
while (current) {
  console.log(current.data);
  current = current.next;
}

console.log("Second Sorted Linked List:");
current = list2;
while (current) {
  console.log(current.data);
  current = current.next;
}

let mergedList = mergeTwoSortedLists(list1, list2);

console.log("Merged Sorted Linked List:");
current = mergedList;
while (current) {
  console.log(current.data);
  current = current.next;
}
```

Implement Hash Table (Hash Map)

```
class HashTable {
 constructor(size = 10) {
  this.size = size;
  this.table = new Array(size);
 }

 _hash(key) {
  let hash = 0;
  for (let char of key) {
   hash = (hash + char.charCodeAt(0)) % this.size;
  }
  return hash;
 }

 set(key, value) {
  const index = this._hash(key);
  if (!this.table[index]) {
   this.table[index] = [];
  }
  this.table[index].push([key, value]);
 }

 get(key) {
  const index = this._hash(key);
  if (!this.table[index]) return undefined;
  for (let entry of this.table[index]) {
   if (entry[0] === key) {
    return entry[1];
   }
  }
```

```
    return undefined;
  }

  remove(key) {
    const index = this._hash(key);
    if (!this.table[index]) return false;
    this.table[index] = this.table[index].filter(entry => entry[0] !== key);
    return true;
  }
}

// Example usage of Hash Table
let hashTable = new HashTable();

hashTable.set("name", "John");
hashTable.set("age", 30);
hashTable.set("city", "New York");

console.log("Value for 'name':", hashTable.get("name"));
console.log("Value for 'age':", hashTable.get("age"));

hashTable.remove("age");
console.log("Value for 'age' after removal:", hashTable.get("age"));
```

Implement Set Data Structure

```
class Set {
  constructor() {
    this.items = {};
  }

  add(element) {
```

```
    if (!this.has(element)) {
      this.items[element] = element;
      return true;
    }
    return false;
  }

  delete(element) {
    if (this.has(element)) {
      delete this.items[element];
      return true;
    }
    return false;
  }

  has(element) {
    return Object.prototype.hasOwnProperty.call(this.items, element);
  }

  size() {
    return Object.keys(this.items).length;
  }

  values() {
    return Object.values(this.items);
  }

  clear() {
    this.items = {};
  }
}
```

```
// Example usage of Set
let set = new Set();

set.add(10);
set.add(20);
set.add(30);

console.log("Set values:", set.values());

set.delete(20);
console.log("Set values after deletion:", set.values());
```

Implement Priority Queue

```
class PriorityQueue {
  constructor() {
    this.queue = [];
  }
  enqueue(element, priority) {
    this.queue.push({ element, priority });
    this.sortQueue();
  }

  dequeue() {
    return this.queue.shift().element;
  }

  sortQueue() {
    this.queue.sort((a, b) => a.priority - b.priority);
  }
```

```
  isEmpty() {
    return this.queue.length === 0;
  }
}

// Example usage of Priority Queue
let priorityQueue = new PriorityQueue();

priorityQueue.enqueue("Task 1", 3);
priorityQueue.enqueue("Task 2", 1);
priorityQueue.enqueue("Task 3", 2);

while (!priorityQueue.isEmpty()) {
  console.log(priorityQueue.dequeue());
}
```

Validate Email Address

```
function isValidEmailAddress(email) {
  const pattern = /^[^\s@]+@[^\s@]+\.[^\s@]+$/;
  return pattern.test(email);
}

let email = "test@example.com"; // Change the email address here
if (isValidEmailAddress(email)) {
  console.log(`${email} is a valid email address`);
} else {
  console.log(`${email} is not a valid email address`);
}
```

Validate Password Strength

```
function isStrongPassword(password) {
  const pattern = /^(?=.*[a-z])(?=.*[A-Z])(?=.*\d)[a-zA-Z\d]{8,}$/;
  return pattern.test(password);
}

let password = "Abcde123"; // Change the password here
if (isStrongPassword(password)) {
  console.log(`${password} is a strong password`);
} else {
  console.log(`${password} is not a strong password`);
}
```

Validate Credit Card Number

```
function isValidCreditCardNumber(cardNumber) {
  const pattern = /^\d{4}-\d{4}-\d{4}-\d{4}$/;
  return pattern.test(cardNumber);
}

let cardNumber = "1234-5678-9012-3456"; // Change the credit card number here
if (isValidCreditCardNumber(cardNumber)) {
  console.log(`${cardNumber} is a valid credit card number`);
} else {
  console.log(`${cardNumber} is not a valid credit card number`);
}
```

Generate Random Password

```
function generateRandomPassword(length) {
  const charset =
"abcdefghijklmnopqrstuvwxyzABCDEFGHIJKLMNOPQRSTUVWXYZ0123456789!
@#$%^&*()-_=+";
```

```
  let password = "";
  for (let i = 0; i < length; i++) {
    const randomIndex = Math.floor(Math.random() * charset.length);
    password += charset[randomIndex];
  }
  return password;
}

let passwordLength = 12; // Change the desired length of the password here
let randomPassword = generateRandomPassword(passwordLength);
console.log("Random Password:", randomPassword);
```

Convert Decimal to Binary

```
function decimalToBinary(decimal) {
  return (decimal >>> 0).toString(2); // Using bitwise operator to convert to unsigned
binary
}

let decimalNumber = 10; // Change the decimal number here
let binaryNumber = decimalToBinary(decimalNumber);
console.log("Binary representation:", binaryNumber);
```

Convert Binary to Decimal

```
function binaryToDecimal(binary) {
  return parseInt(binary, 2);
}

let binaryNumber = "1010"; // Change the binary number here
let decimalNumber = binaryToDecimal(binaryNumber);
console.log("Decimal representation:", decimalNumber);
```

Convert Decimal to Octal

```
function decimalToOctal(decimal) {
  return (decimal >>> 0).toString(8); // Using bitwise operator to convert to unsigned
octal
}

let decimalNumber = 23; // Change the decimal number here
let octalNumber = decimalToOctal(decimalNumber);
console.log("Octal representation:", octalNumber);
```

Convert Decimal to Hexadecimal

```
function decimalToHexadecimal(decimal) {
  return (decimal >>> 0).toString(16).toUpperCase(); // Using bitwise operator to
convert to unsigned hexadecimal
}
let decimalNumber = 255; // Change the decimal number here
let hexadecimalNumber = decimalToHexadecimal(decimalNumber);
console.log("Hexadecimal representation:", hexadecimalNumber);
```

Convert Binary to Octal

```
function binaryToOctal(binary) {
  let decimal = parseInt(binary, 2);
  return (decimal >>> 0).toString(8); // Using bitwise operator to convert to unsigned
octal
}
let binaryNumber = "101010"; // Change the binary number here
let octalNumber = binaryToOctal(binaryNumber);
console.log("Octal representation:", octalNumber);
```

Convert Binary to Hexadecimal

```
function binaryToHexadecimal(binary) {
```

```
  let decimal = parseInt(binary, 2);
  return (decimal >>> 0).toString(16).toUpperCase(); // Using bitwise operator to
convert to unsigned hexadecimal
}
let binaryNumber = "110011"; // Change the binary number here
let hexadecimalNumber = binaryToHexadecimal(binaryNumber);
console.log("Hexadecimal representation:", hexadecimalNumber);
```

Convert Octal to Binary

```
function octalToBinary(octal) {
  let decimal = parseInt(octal, 8);
  return (decimal >>> 0).toString(2); // Using bitwise operator to convert to unsigned
binary
}

let octalNumber = "36"; // Change the octal number here
let binaryNumber = octalToBinary(octalNumber);
console.log("Binary representation:", binaryNumber);
```

Convert Octal to Decimal

```
function octalToDecimal(octal) {
  return parseInt(octal, 8);
}

let octalNumber = "36"; // Change the octal number here
let decimalNumber = octalToDecimal(octalNumber);
console.log("Decimal representation:", decimalNumber);
```

Convert Octal to Hexadecimal

```
function octalToHexadecimal(octal) {
  let decimal = parseInt(octal, 8);
```

```
  return (decimal >>> 0).toString(16).toUpperCase(); // Using bitwise operator to
convert to unsigned hexadecimal
}

let octalNumber = "36"; // Change the octal number here
let hexadecimalNumber = octalToHexadecimal(octalNumber);
console.log("Hexadecimal representation:", hexadecimalNumber);
```

Convert Hexadecimal to Binary

```
function hexadecimalToBinary(hexadecimal) {
  let decimal = parseInt(hexadecimal, 16);
  return (decimal >>> 0).toString(2); // Using bitwise operator to convert to unsigned
binary
}

let hexadecimalNumber = "FF"; // Change the hexadecimal number here
let binaryNumber = hexadecimalToBinary(hexadecimalNumber);
console.log("Binary representation:", binaryNumber);
```

Convert Hexadecimal to Decimal

```
function hexadecimalToDecimal(hexadecimal) {
  return parseInt(hexadecimal, 16);
}
let hexadecimalNumber = "FF"; // Change the hexadecimal number here
let decimalNumber = hexadecimalToDecimal(hexadecimalNumber);
console.log("Decimal representation:", decimalNumber);
```

Convert Hexadecimal to Octal

```
function hexadecimalToOctal(hexadecimal) {
  let decimal = parseInt(hexadecimal, 16);
```

```
  return (decimal >>> 0).toString(8); // Using bitwise operator to convert to unsigned
octal
}

let hexadecimalNumber = "1A"; // Change the hexadecimal number here
let octalNumber = hexadecimalToOctal(hexadecimalNumber);
console.log("Octal representation:", octalNumber);
```

Implement Caesar Cipher

```
function caesarCipher(text, shift) {
  return text
    .split("")
    .map(char => {
      if (char.match(/[a-zA-Z]/)) {
        let code = char.charCodeAt(0);
        let base = code >= 97 ? 97 : 65;
        return String.fromCharCode(base + ((code - base + shift) % 26));
      }
      return char;
    })
    .join("");
}

let plaintext = "Hello, World!";
let encryptedText = caesarCipher(plaintext, 3);
console.log("Encrypted Text:", encryptedText);

let decryptedText = caesarCipher(encryptedText, -3);
console.log("Decrypted Text:", decryptedText);
```

Implement Vigenère Cipher

```
function vigenereCipher(text, key) {
 let keyIndex = 0;
 return text
  .split("")
  .map(char => {
   if (char.match(/[a-zA-Z]/)) {
    let shift = key[keyIndex].toUpperCase().charCodeAt(0) - 65;
    let code = char.charCodeAt(0);
    let base = code >= 97 ? 97 : 65;
    let encryptedChar = String.fromCharCode(base + ((code - base + shift) % 26));
    keyIndex = (keyIndex + 1) % key.length;
    return encryptedChar;
   }
   return char;
  })
  .join("");
}

let plaintext = "Hello, World!";
let key = "KEY";
let encryptedText = vigenereCipher(plaintext, key);
console.log("Encrypted Text:", encryptedText);

let decryptedText = vigenereCipher(encryptedText, key);
console.log("Decrypted Text:", decryptedText);
```

Implement ROT13 Cipher

```
function rot13Cipher(text) {
 return text
  .split("")
```

```
    .map(char => {
      if (char.match(/[a-zA-Z]/)) {
        let code = char.charCodeAt(0);
        let base = code >= 97 ? 97 : 65;
        return String.fromCharCode(base + ((code - base + 13) % 26));
      }
      return char;
    })
    .join("");
}
let plaintext = "Hello, World!";
let encryptedText = rot13Cipher(plaintext);
console.log("Encrypted Text:", encryptedText);
let decryptedText = rot13Cipher(encryptedText); // Rot13 is its own inverse
console.log("Decrypted Text:", decryptedText);
```

Implement Bubble Sort Animation

```
function bubbleSortAnimation(arr) {
  let steps = [];
  let n = arr.length;
  for (let i = 0; i < n - 1; i++) {
    for (let j = 0; j < n - i - 1; j++) {
      // Compare arr[j] and arr[j + 1]
      if (arr[j] > arr[j + 1]) {
        // Swap arr[j] and arr[j + 1]
        [arr[j], arr[j + 1]] = [arr[j + 1], arr[j]];
        // Store the state of the array after each swap
        steps.push([...arr]);
      }
    }
  }
```

```
  return steps;
}
// Example usage of Bubble Sort Animation
let array = [5, 3, 8, 1, 4];
let sortSteps = bubbleSortAnimation(array);
console.log("Bubble Sort Animation Steps:", sortSteps);
```

Implement Tic-Tac-Toe Game

```
class TicTacToe {
  constructor() {
    this.board = Array(9).fill(null);
    this.currentPlayer = "X";
    this.winningCombinations = [
      [0, 1, 2], [3, 4, 5], [6, 7, 8], // Rows
      [0, 3, 6], [1, 4, 7], [2, 5, 8], // Columns
      [0, 4, 8], [2, 4, 6] // Diagonals
    ];
    this.winner = null;
    this.moves = 0;
  }
  makeMove(index) {
    if (this.board[index] === null && !this.winner) {
      this.board[index] = this.currentPlayer;
      this.moves++;
      this.checkWinner();
      this.currentPlayer = this.currentPlayer === "X" ? "O" : "X";
    }
  }
  checkWinner() {
    for (let combination of this.winningCombinations) {
      const [a, b, c] = combination;
```

```
    if (this.board[a] && this.board[a] === this.board[b] && this.board[a] ===
this.board[c]) {
      this.winner = this.board[a];
      break;
    }
  }
 }

 isDraw() {
  return this.moves === 9 && !this.winner;
 }

 isGameOver() {
  return this.winner !== null || this.isDraw();
 }
}

// Example usage of Tic-Tac-Toe Game
let game = new TicTacToe();
game.makeMove(0);
game.makeMove(4);
game.makeMove(1);
game.makeMove(3);
game.makeMove(2);
console.log("Winner:", game.winner);
console.log("Is Draw:", game.isDraw());
console.log("Is Game Over:", game.isGameOver());
```

Implement Snake Game

// Implementation of Snake Game can be complex and requires more code. Below is a simplified version:

```
class SnakeGame {
 constructor() {
  this.board = Array(10).fill().map(() => Array(10).fill(0));
  this.snake = [{ x: 0, y: 0 }];
  this.food = { x: Math.floor(Math.random() * 10), y: Math.floor(Math.random() * 10)
};
  this.direction = "right";
 }

 move() {
  const head = this.snake[0];
  const newHead = { x: head.x, y: head.y };

  if (this.direction === "right") {
   newHead.y++;
  } else if (this.direction === "left") {
   newHead.y--;
  } else if (this.direction === "up") {
   newHead.x--;
  } else if (this.direction === "down") {
   newHead.x++;
  }

  if (newHead.x < 0 || newHead.x >= 10 || newHead.y < 0 || newHead.y >= 10) {
   return false; // Game over (out of bounds)
  }

  this.snake.unshift(newHead);

  if (newHead.x === this.food.x && newHead.y === this.food.y) {
```

```
      this.food = { x: Math.floor(Math.random() * 10), y: Math.floor(Math.random() * 10)
};
    } else {
      this.snake.pop();
    }

    return true; // Game continues
  }
}
// Example usage of Snake Game
let snakeGame = new SnakeGame();
console.log("Initial Snake Position:", snakeGame.snake);
snakeGame.move();
console.log("Snake Position after Move:", snakeGame.snake);
```

Implement Memory Matching Game

```
// Implementation of Memory Matching Game can be more complex and requires UI
interactions.

// Below is a simplified version of the logic:

class MemoryMatchingGame {
  constructor(cards) {
    this.cards = [...cards, ...cards];
    this.shuffleCards();
    this.selectedCards = [];
  }

  shuffleCards() {
    for (let i = this.cards.length - 1; i > 0; i--) {
      const j = Math.floor(Math.random() * (i + 1));
```

```
      [this.cards[i], this.cards[j]] = [this.cards[j], this.cards[i]];
    }
  }

  selectCard(index) {
    if (this.selectedCards.length < 2 && !this.selectedCards.includes(index)) {
      this.selectedCards.push(index);
      if (this.selectedCards.length === 2) {
        const [firstIndex, secondIndex] = this.selectedCards;
        if (this.cards[firstIndex] !== this.cards[secondIndex]) {
          // If not matched, deselect after a delay (simulation)
          setTimeout(() => {
            this.selectedCards = [];
          }, 1000);
        } else {
          // If matched, keep selected
        }
      }
    }
  }

  isGameOver() {
    return this.cards.every((card, index) => this.selectedCards.includes(index));
  }
}
// Example usage of Memory Matching Game
let game = new MemoryMatchingGame(["A", "B", "C", "D"]);
game.selectCard(0);
game.selectCard(3);
game.selectCard(1);
game.selectCard(2);
```

```
console.log("Game Over:", game.isGameOver());
```

Implement Blackjack Game

```
// Implementation of Blackjack Game can be complex and requires more code.
// Below is a simplified version of the logic:
class BlackjackGame {
  constructor() {
    this.deck = this.createDeck();
    this.shuffleDeck();
    this.playerHand = [];
    this.dealerHand = [];
    this.dealInitialCards();
  }

  createDeck() {
    const suits = ["Hearts", "Diamonds", "Clubs", "Spades"];
    const ranks = ["2", "3", "4", "5", "6", "7", "8", "9", "10", "J", "Q", "K", "A"];
    const deck = [];
    for (let suit of suits) {
      for (let rank of ranks) {
        deck.push(`${rank} of ${suit}`);
      }
    }
    return deck;
  }

  shuffleDeck() {
    for (let i = this.deck.length - 1; i > 0; i--) {
      const j = Math.floor(Math.random() * (i + 1));
      [this.deck[i], this.deck[j]] = [this.deck[j], this.deck[i]];
    }
```

```
}

dealInitialCards() {
  this.playerHand.push(this.deck.pop());
  this.dealerHand.push(this.deck.pop());
  this.playerHand.push(this.deck.pop());
  this.dealerHand.push(this.deck.pop());
}

hit(player) {
  player.push(this.deck.pop());
}

calculateHandValue(hand) {
  let value = 0;
  let aceCount = 0;
  for (let card of hand) {
    let rank = card.split(" ")[0];
    if (rank === "A") {
      aceCount++;
      value += 11;
    } else if (["J", "Q", "K"].includes(rank)) {
      value += 10;
    } else {
      value += parseInt(rank);
    }
  }
  while (value > 21 && aceCount > 0) {
    value -= 10;
    aceCount--;
  }
```

```
    return value;
  }

  isBust(hand) {
    return this.calculateHandValue(hand) > 21;
  }

  isBlackjack(hand) {
    return hand.length === 2 && this.calculateHandValue(hand) === 21;
  }

  isGameOver() {
    return this.isBust(this.playerHand) || this.isBust(this.dealerHand) ||
this.playerHand.length === 5;
  }
}

// Example usage of Blackjack Game
let blackjackGame = new BlackjackGame();
console.log("Player Hand:", blackjackGame.playerHand);
console.log("Dealer Hand:", blackjackGame.dealerHand);
blackjackGame.hit(blackjackGame.playerHand);
console.log("Player Hand after Hit:", blackjackGame.playerHand);
console.log("Player Hand Value:",
blackjackGame.calculateHandValue(blackjackGame.playerHand));
console.log("Is Player Bust:", blackjackGame.isBust(blackjackGame.playerHand));
console.log("Is Player Blackjack:",
blackjackGame.isBlackjack(blackjackGame.playerHand));
console.log("Is Game Over:", blackjackGame.isGameOver());
```

Implement Quiz Game

```
// Implementation of Quiz Game can be more complex and requires UI interactions.
// Below is a simplified version of the logic:
class QuizGame {
  constructor(questions) {
    this.questions = questions;
    this.currentQuestionIndex = 0;
    this.score = 0;
  }
  displayCurrentQuestion() {
    console.log(this.questions[this.currentQuestionIndex].question);
    console.log("Options:");
    this.questions[this.currentQuestionIndex].options.forEach((option, index) => {
      console.log(`${index + 1}. ${option}`);
    });
  }
  answerCurrentQuestion(answerIndex) {
    if (answerIndex >= 0 && answerIndex <
this.questions[this.currentQuestionIndex].options.length) {
      if (this.questions[this.currentQuestionIndex].correctIndex === answerIndex) {
        console.log("Correct answer!");
        this.score++;
      } else {
        console.log("Incorrect answer!");
      }
      this.currentQuestionIndex++;
      if (this.currentQuestionIndex < this.questions.length) {
        this.displayCurrentQuestion();
      } else {
        this.displayResult();
      }
```

```
    } else {
      console.log("Invalid answer index!");
    }
  }
  displayResult() {
    console.log("Quiz Over!");
    console.log(`Your Score: ${this.score} out of ${this.questions.length}`);
  }
}
// Example usage of Quiz Game
let questions = [
  {
    question: "What is the capital of France?",
    options: ["Paris", "London", "Berlin", "Madrid"],
    correctIndex: 0
  },
  {
    question: "Which planet is known as the Red Planet?",
    options: ["Mars", "Jupiter", "Earth", "Venus"],
    correctIndex: 0
  },
  {
    question: "Who painted the Mona Lisa?",
    options: ["Leonardo da Vinci", "Pablo Picasso", "Vincent van Gogh", "Claude
Monet"],
    correctIndex: 0
  }
];
let quizGame = new QuizGame(questions);
quizGame.displayCurrentQuestion();
quizGame.answerCurrentQuestion(0);
```

```
quizGame.answerCurrentQuestion(1);
quizGame.answerCurrentQuestion(0);
```

Implement Weather Application (API Integration)

```
// Sample implementation of a Weather Application using OpenWeatherMap API
const apiKey = 'YOUR_API_KEY'; // Replace with your API key
const city = 'New York';
const apiUrl =
`https://api.openweathermap.org/data/2.5/weather?q=${city}&appid=${apiKey}&units=
metric`;
fetch(apiUrl)
  .then(response => response.json())
  .then(data => {
    console.log(`Weather in ${city}:`);
    console.log(`Temperature: ${data.main.temp} °C`);
    console.log(`Description: ${data.weather[0].description}`);
  })
  .catch(error => {
    console.log('Error fetching weather data:', error);
  });
```

Implement To-Do List Application

```
// Sample implementation of a To-Do List Application using localStorage
let todos = [];
function addTodoItem(item) {
  todos.push({ id: todos.length + 1, task: item, completed: false });
  updateLocalStorage();
}
function toggleTodoItem(id) {
  const index = todos.findIndex(todo => todo.id === id);
  if (index !== -1) {
```

```
    todos[index].completed = !todos[index].completed;
    updateLocalStorage();
  }
}
function removeTodoItem(id) {
  todos = todos.filter(todo => todo.id !== id);
  updateLocalStorage();
}
function updateLocalStorage() {
  localStorage.setItem('todos', JSON.stringify(todos));
}
// Example usage of To-Do List Application
addTodoItem('Buy groceries');
addTodoItem('Finish homework');
toggleTodoItem(1);
removeTodoItem(2);
console.log('To-Do List:', todos);
```

Implement Calendar Application

```
// Sample implementation of a Calendar Application using Date object
function displayCalendar(year, month) {
  const firstDay = new Date(year, month - 1, 1).getDay();
  const daysInMonth = new Date(year, month, 0).getDate();
  const calendar = [];
  let day = 1;
  for (let i = 0; i < 6; i++) {
    const week = [];
    for (let j = 0; j < 7; j++) {
      if (i === 0 && j < firstDay) {
        week.push('');
      } else if (day > daysInMonth) {
```

```
        break;
      } else {
        week.push(day++);
      }
    }
    calendar.push(week);
    if (day > daysInMonth) {
      break;
    }
  }

  console.log(`Calendar for ${month}/${year}:`);
  console.log(calendar);
}

// Example usage of Calendar Application
displayCalendar(2024, 4); // Display calendar for April 2024
```

Implement Chat Application (using WebSockets)

```
// Sample implementation of a Chat Application using WebSocket
const WebSocketServer = require('ws').Server;
const wss = new WebSocketServer({ port: 8080 });
wss.on('connection', ws => {
  console.log('Client connected');
  ws.on('message', message => {
    console.log(`Received message: ${message}`);
    // Broadcast received message to all clients
    wss.clients.forEach(client => {
      if (client !== ws && client.readyState === WebSocket.OPEN) {
        client.send(message);
      }
```

```
    });
  });

  ws.on('close', () => {
    console.log('Client disconnected');
  });
});
console.log('WebSocket server listening on port 8080');
```

Implement Calculator

```
// Sample implementation of a basic calculator
function add(a, b) {
  return a + b;
}

function subtract(a, b) {
  return a - b;
}

function multiply(a, b) {
  return a * b;
}

function divide(a, b) {
  if (b === 0) {
    return 'Error: Division by zero';
  }
  return a / b;
}

// Example usage of Calculator
```

```
console.log('Addition:', add(5, 3));
console.log('Subtraction:', subtract(5, 3));
console.log('Multiplication:', multiply(5, 3));
console.log('Division:', divide(5, 0));
```

Implement Currency Converter

```
// Sample implementation of a Currency Converter using exchange rates
const exchangeRates = {
  USD: 1.0,
  EUR: 0.85,
  GBP: 0.73,
  JPY: 111.23,
  CNY: 6.45
};

function convertCurrency(amount, fromCurrency, toCurrency) {
  if (fromCurrency === toCurrency) {
    return amount;
  }
  const equivalentAmount = amount / exchangeRates[fromCurrency];
  return equivalentAmount * exchangeRates[toCurrency];
}

// Example usage of Currency Converter
const amount = 100;
const fromCurrency = 'USD';
const toCurrency = 'EUR';
console.log(`${amount} ${fromCurrency} = ${convertCurrency(amount, fromCurrency,
toCurrency)} ${toCurrency}`);
```

Implement Countdown Timer

```
// Sample implementation of a Countdown Timer
function countdownTimer(seconds) {
  let remainingSeconds = seconds;
  const intervalId = setInterval(() => {
    if (remainingSeconds > 0) {
      console.log(`Time remaining: ${remainingSeconds} seconds`);
      remainingSeconds--;
    } else {
      clearInterval(intervalId);
      console.log('Countdown complete!');
    }
  }, 1000);
}

// Example usage of Countdown Timer
countdownTimer(10); // Start a countdown timer for 10 seconds
```

Implement Stopwatch

```
// Sample implementation of a Stopwatch

class Stopwatch {
  constructor() {
    this.startTime = 0;
    this.elapsedTime = 0;
    this.isRunning = false;
  }

  start() {
    if (!this.isRunning) {
      this.startTime = Date.now() - this.elapsedTime;
```

```
      this.isRunning = true;
      this.update();
    }
  }

  stop() {
    if (this.isRunning) {
      clearInterval(this.intervalId);
      this.isRunning = false;
    }
  }

  reset() {
    this.stop();
    this.elapsedTime = 0;
  }

  update() {
    this.intervalId = setInterval(() => {
      this.elapsedTime = Date.now() - this.startTime;
      console.log(`Elapsed time: ${this.elapsedTime / 1000} seconds`);
    }, 100);
  }
}

// Example usage of Stopwatch
let stopwatch = new Stopwatch();
stopwatch.start(); // Start the stopwatch
setTimeout(() => {
  stopwatch.stop(); // Stop the stopwatch after 3 seconds
}, 3000);
```

Implement Pomodoro Timer

```
// Sample implementation of a Pomodoro Timer

class PomodoroTimer {
  constructor(workDuration, breakDuration) {
    this.workDuration = workDuration * 60 * 1000; // in milliseconds
    this.breakDuration = breakDuration * 60 * 1000; // in milliseconds
    this.isWorking = true;
    this.isRunning = false;
    this.timerId = null;
  }

  startTimer() {
    if (!this.isRunning) {
      this.isRunning = true;
      this.timerId = setInterval(() => {
        if (this.isWorking) {
          console.log('Work time remaining:', this.formatTime(this.workDuration));
          this.workDuration -= 1000;
          if (this.workDuration < 0) {
            clearInterval(this.timerId);
            console.log('Work session ended. Take a break!');
            this.isWorking = false;
            this.startTimer();
          }
        } else {
          console.log('Break time remaining:', this.formatTime(this.breakDuration));
          this.breakDuration -= 1000;
          if (this.breakDuration < 0) {
            clearInterval(this.timerId);
            console.log('Break session ended. Back to work!');
```

```
          this.isWorking = true;
          this.startTimer();
        }
      }
    }, 1000);
  }
}

stopTimer() {
  if (this.isRunning) {
    clearInterval(this.timerId);
    this.isRunning = false;
    console.log('Timer stopped.');
  }
}

formatTime(milliseconds) {
  const totalSeconds = Math.floor(milliseconds / 1000);
  const minutes = Math.floor(totalSeconds / 60);
  const seconds = totalSeconds % 60;
  return `${minutes.toString().padStart(2, '0')}:${seconds.toString().padStart(2, '0')}`;
}
}

// Example usage of Pomodoro Timer
let pomodoro = new PomodoroTimer(25, 5);
pomodoro.startTimer(); // Start the Pomodoro Timer
```

Implement Music Player

```
// Sample implementation of a Music Player

class MusicPlayer {
 constructor() {
  this.playlist = [];
  this.currentTrackIndex = -1;
  this.isPlaying = false;
 }

 addTrack(track) {
  this.playlist.push(track);
 }

 play() {
  if (this.playlist.length > 0 && !this.isPlaying) {
   this.isPlaying = true;
   this.currentTrackIndex = 0;
   console.log(`Now playing: ${this.playlist[this.currentTrackIndex]}`);
  }
 }

 pause() {
  if (this.isPlaying) {
   this.isPlaying = false;
   console.log('Music paused.');
  }
 }

 nextTrack() {
  if (this.playlist.length > 0 && this.currentTrackIndex < this.playlist.length - 1) {
```

```
      this.currentTrackIndex++;
      console.log(`Now playing: ${this.playlist[this.currentTrackIndex]}`);
    } else {
      console.log('End of playlist.');
    }
  }

  previousTrack() {
    if (this.playlist.length > 0 && this.currentTrackIndex > 0) {
      this.currentTrackIndex--;
      console.log(`Now playing: ${this.playlist[this.currentTrackIndex]}`);
    } else {
      console.log('Beginning of playlist.');
    }
  }
}

// Example usage of Music Player
let musicPlayer = new MusicPlayer();
musicPlayer.addTrack('Song 1');
musicPlayer.addTrack('Song 2');
musicPlayer.addTrack('Song 3');
musicPlayer.play(); // Play the music
musicPlayer.nextTrack(); // Play the next track
musicPlayer.pause(); // Pause the music
```

Implement Video Player

```
// Sample implementation of a Video Player
class VideoPlayer {
  constructor() {
    this.videoUrl = null;
```

```
    this.isPlaying = false;
    this.currentTime = 0;
  }

  load(videoUrl) {
    this.videoUrl = videoUrl;
    console.log(`Video loaded: ${this.videoUrl}`);
  }

  play() {
    if (this.videoUrl && !this.isPlaying) {
      this.isPlaying = true;
      console.log('Video playing...');
    }
  }

  pause() {
    if (this.isPlaying) {
      this.isPlaying = false;
      console.log('Video paused.');
    }
  }

  seek(seconds) {
    if (this.isPlaying) {
      this.currentTime = seconds;
      console.log(`Seeking to ${seconds} seconds`);
    }
  }
}
```

```
// Example usage of Video Player
let videoPlayer = new VideoPlayer();
videoPlayer.load('https://example.com/video.mp4');
videoPlayer.play(); // Play the video
videoPlayer.seek(30); // Seek to 30 seconds
videoPlayer.pause(); // Pause the video
```

Implement Image Slider

```
// Sample implementation of an Image Slider
class ImageSlider {
  constructor(images) {
    this.images = images;
    this.currentIndex = 0;
  }

  showCurrentImage() {
    console.log(`Showing image: ${this.images[this.currentIndex]}`);
  }

  nextImage() {
    if (this.currentIndex < this.images.length - 1) {
      this.currentIndex++;
    } else {
      this.currentIndex = 0;
    }
    this.showCurrentImage();
  }

  previousImage() {
    if (this.currentIndex > 0) {
      this.currentIndex--;
```

```
    } else {
      this.currentIndex = this.images.length - 1;
    }
    this.showCurrentImage();
  }
}

// Example usage of Image Slider
let imageSlider = new ImageSlider(['image1.jpg', 'image2.jpg', 'image3.jpg']);
imageSlider.showCurrentImage(); // Show the first image
imageSlider.nextImage(); // Show the next image
imageSlider.previousImage(); // Show the previous image
```

Implement File Uploader

```
// Sample implementation of a File Uploader
class FileUploader {
  constructor() {
    this.files = [];
  }

  uploadFile(file) {
    this.files.push(file);
    console.log(`File uploaded: ${file}`);
  }

  listUploadedFiles() {
    console.log('Uploaded files:');
    this.files.forEach((file, index) => {
      console.log(`${index + 1}. ${file}`);
    });
  }
```

```
}

// Example usage of File Uploader
let fileUploader = new FileUploader();
fileUploader.uploadFile('document.pdf');
fileUploader.uploadFile('image.jpg');
fileUploader.listUploadedFiles(); // List uploaded files
```

Implement Drawing Application

```
// Sample implementation of a Drawing Application using Canvas
const canvas = document.createElement('canvas');
canvas.width = 800;
canvas.height = 600;
document.body.appendChild(canvas);

const ctx = canvas.getContext('2d');
let isDrawing = false;
let lastX = 0;
let lastY = 0;

canvas.addEventListener('mousedown', startDrawing);
canvas.addEventListener('mousemove', draw);
canvas.addEventListener('mouseup', stopDrawing);
canvas.addEventListener('mouseout', stopDrawing);

function startDrawing(e) {
  isDrawing = true;
  [lastX, lastY] = [e.offsetX, e.offsetY];
}

function draw(e) {
```

```
  if (isDrawing) {
    ctx.beginPath();
    ctx.moveTo(lastX, lastY);
    ctx.lineTo(e.offsetX, e.offsetY);
    ctx.stroke();
    [lastX, lastY] = [e.offsetX, e.offsetY];
  }
}

function stopDrawing() {
  isDrawing = false;
}

// Example usage of Drawing Application: Draw on the canvas
```

Implement Markdown Editor

```
// Sample implementation of a Markdown Editor using a textarea
const markdownTextarea = document.createElement('textarea');
markdownTextarea.rows = 10;
markdownTextarea.cols = 50;
document.body.appendChild(markdownTextarea);

markdownTextarea.addEventListener('input', () => {
  const markdownContent = markdownTextarea.value;
  const markdownHtml = marked(markdownContent); // Assuming 'marked' library is
included
  document.getElementById('preview').innerHTML = markdownHtml;
});

// Example usage of Markdown Editor: Edit Markdown content in the textarea
```

Implement Code Editor

```
// Sample implementation of a Code Editor using CodeMirror library
const editorContainer = document.createElement('div');
document.body.appendChild(editorContainer);

const codeEditor = CodeMirror(editorContainer, {
  value: 'function greet(name) {\n  return `Hello, ${name}!`;\n}',
  mode: 'javascript',
  lineNumbers: true
});

// Example usage of Code Editor: Edit and display JavaScript code
```

Implement CRUD Operations (using Local Storage)

javascript

Copy code

```
// Sample implementation of CRUD operations using Local Storage

class LocalStorageCRUD {
  constructor(storageKey) {
    this.storageKey = storageKey;
    this.items = JSON.parse(localStorage.getItem(this.storageKey)) || [];
  }

  create(item) {
    this.items.push(item);
    this.saveItems();
  }

  read() {
    return this.items;
  }
```

```
  update(index, newItem) {
    if (index >= 0 && index < this.items.length) {
      this.items[index] = newItem;
      this.saveItems();
    }
  }

  delete(index) {
    if (index >= 0 && index < this.items.length) {
      this.items.splice(index, 1);
      this.saveItems();
    }
  }

  saveItems() {
    localStorage.setItem(this.storageKey, JSON.stringify(this.items));
  }
}

// Example usage of LocalStorageCRUD for managing items
const todoList = new LocalStorageCRUD('todos');
todoList.create({ id: 1, task: 'Buy groceries', completed: false });
console.log('Current todos:', todoList.read());
todoList.update(0, { id: 1, task: 'Buy milk', completed: false });
console.log('Updated todos:', todoList.read());
todoList.delete(0);
console.log('Remaining todos:', todoList.read());
```

Implement Authentication System

```
// Sample implementation of an Authentication System using Local Storage
class AuthenticationService {
 constructor() {
  this.isAuthenticated = false;
  this.currentUser = null;
 }

 login(username, password) {
  // Example: Check credentials against stored data (e.g., from Local Storage)
  const storedUsername = localStorage.getItem('username');
  const storedPassword = localStorage.getItem('password');
  if (username === storedUsername && password === storedPassword) {
   this.isAuthenticated = true;
   this.currentUser = username;
   console.log('Login successful!');
  } else {
   console.log('Invalid credentials. Login failed.');
  }
 }

 logout() {
  this.isAuthenticated = false;
  this.currentUser = null;
  console.log('Logout successful.');
 }

 isAuthenticated() {
  return this.isAuthenticated;
 }
```

```
  getCurrentUser() {
    return this.currentUser;
  }
}

// Example usage of AuthenticationService for user authentication
const authService = new AuthenticationService();
authService.login('user123', 'password123');
console.log('Authenticated:', authService.isAuthenticated);
console.log('Current User:', authService.getCurrentUser());
authService.logout();
console.log('Authenticated:', authService.isAuthenticated);
```

Implement Role-based Access Control

```
// Sample implementation of Role-based Access Control (RBAC)
const roles = {
  admin: ['read', 'write', 'delete'],
  editor: ['read', 'write'],
  guest: ['read']
};

function hasPermission(role, permission) {
  return roles[role].includes(permission);
}

// Example usage of Role-based Access Control
const userRole = 'editor';
console.log('Has read permission:', hasPermission(userRole, 'read'));
console.log('Has write permission:', hasPermission(userRole, 'write'));
console.log('Has delete permission:', hasPermission(userRole, 'delete'));
```

Implement JWT Authentication

```
// Sample implementation of JWT Authentication
const jwt = require('jsonwebtoken');

const secretKey = 'secret';

function generateToken(payload) {
  return jwt.sign(payload, secretKey);
}

function verifyToken(token) {
  try {
    return jwt.verify(token, secretKey);
  } catch (error) {
    console.log('Token verification failed:', error.message);
    return null;
  }
}

// Example usage of JWT Authentication
const user = { id: 123, username: 'user123' };
const token = generateToken(user);
console.log('Generated Token:', token);
const decodedUser = verifyToken(token);
console.log('Decoded User:', decodedUser);
```

Implement Social Media Login (e.g., Google, Facebook)

```
// Sample implementation of Social Media Login (using OAuth)
function socialMediaLogin(provider) {
  // Redirect user to OAuth provider login page
  window.location.href = `https://example.com/${provider}/login`;
```

```
}
// Example usage of Social Media Login
socialMediaLogin('google'); // Redirect to Google login
socialMediaLogin('facebook'); // Redirect to Facebook login
```

Implement Blogging Platform

```
// Sample implementation of a Blogging Platform

// Define BlogPost class
class BlogPost {
  constructor(title, content, author) {
    this.title = title;
    this.content = content;
    this.author = author;
    this.date = new Date();
  }
}

// Define Blog class
class Blog {
  constructor() {
    this.posts = [];
  }

  addPost(post) {
    this.posts.push(post);
  }

  displayPosts() {
    console.log('--- Blog Posts ---');
    this.posts.forEach((post, index) => {
```

```
      console.log(`Post ${index + 1}: ${post.title} by ${post.author} on ${post.date}`);
      console.log(post.content);
      console.log('---');
    });
  }
}

// Example usage of Blogging Platform
const myBlog = new Blog();
const post1 = new BlogPost('First Post', 'This is my first blog post.', 'John Doe');
const post2 = new BlogPost('Second Post', 'Another interesting post.', 'Jane Smith');
myBlog.addPost(post1);
myBlog.addPost(post2);
myBlog.displayPosts();
```

Implement Portfolio Website

```
// Sample implementation of a Portfolio Website (front-end only)

// HTML structure for Portfolio Website
const portfolioContent = `
  <div>
    <h1>My Portfolio</h1>
    <p>Welcome to my portfolio website!</p>
    <ul>
      <li>Project 1: Description of project 1</li>
      <li>Project 2: Description of project 2</li>
      <li>Project 3: Description of project 3</li>
    </ul>
    <footer>Contact: email@example.com</footer>
  </div>
`;
```

```
// Display Portfolio Website content
document.body.innerHTML = portfolioContent;
```

Implement E-commerce Website

```
// Sample implementation of an E-commerce Website (front-end only)
// HTML structure for E-commerce Website
const ecommerceContent = `
  <div>
    <h1>Our Products</h1>
    <ul>
      <li>Product 1 - $10</li>
      <li>Product 2 - $20</li>
      <li>Product 3 - $30</li>
    </ul>
    <button onclick="addToCart('Product 1', 10)">Add to Cart</button>
    <button onclick="addToCart('Product 2', 20)">Add to Cart</button>
    <button onclick="addToCart('Product 3', 30)">Add to Cart</button>
    <hr>
    <h2>Shopping Cart</h2>
    <ul id="shoppingCart"></ul>
  </div>
`;

// Display E-commerce Website content
document.body.innerHTML = ecommerceContent;

// Function to add item to shopping cart
function addToCart(productName, price) {
  const shoppingCart = document.getElementById('shoppingCart');
  const listItem = document.createElement('li');
```

```
  listItem.textContent = `${productName} - $${price}`;
  shoppingCart.appendChild(listItem);
}
```

Implement Drag and Drop Interface

```
// Sample implementation of a Drag and Drop Interface
// Define drag-and-drop event handlers
function onDragStart(event) {
  event.dataTransfer.setData('text/plain', event.target.id);
}
function onDragOver(event) {
  event.preventDefault();
}

function onDrop(event) {
  const id = event.dataTransfer.getData('text/plain');
  const draggableElement = document.getElementById(id);
  const dropzone = event.target;
  dropzone.appendChild(draggableElement);
}

// Example usage of Drag and Drop Interface
const draggableElement = document.createElement('div');
draggableElement.textContent = 'Drag me!';
draggableElement.id = 'draggable';
draggableElement.draggable = true;
draggableElement.addEventListener('dragstart', onDragStart);

const dropzone = document.createElement('div');
dropzone.textContent = 'Drop here!';
dropzone.id = 'dropzone';
```

```
dropzone.addEventListener('dragover', onDragOver);
dropzone.addEventListener('drop', onDrop);

document.body.appendChild(draggableElement);
document.body.appendChild(dropzone);
```

Implement Responsive Image Gallery

```
// Sample implementation of a Responsive Image Gallery

// CSS styles for Responsive Image Gallery
const galleryStyles = `
  .gallery {
    display: grid;
    grid-template-columns: repeat(auto-fit, minmax(200px, 1fr));
    gap: 10px;
  }

  .gallery img {
    width: 100%;
    height: auto;
  }
`;

// HTML structure for Responsive Image Gallery
const galleryContent = `
  <div class="gallery">
    <img src="image1.jpg" alt="Image 1">
    <img src="image2.jpg" alt="Image 2">
    <img src="image3.jpg" alt="Image 3">
    <!-- Add more images here -->
  </div>
```

```
`;

// Display Responsive Image Gallery
const galleryContainer = document.createElement('div');
galleryContainer.innerHTML = galleryContent;
document.head.insertAdjacentHTML('beforeend', `<style>${galleryStyles}</style>`);
document.body.appendChild(galleryContainer);
```

Implement Real-time Data Dashboard

```
// Sample implementation of a Real-time Data Dashboard using WebSocket

const WebSocket = require('ws');

const wss = new WebSocket.Server({ port: 8080 });

wss.on('connection', ws => {
  console.log('Client connected');

  const intervalId = setInterval(() => {
    const data = Math.random() * 100; // Simulated data
    ws.send(data.toString());
  }, 1000);

  ws.on('close', () => {
    clearInterval(intervalId);
    console.log('Client disconnected');
  });
});

console.log('WebSocket server listening on port 8080');
```

Implement Data Visualization (using D3.js or Chart.js)

```
// Sample implementation of Data Visualization using Chart.js
// Include Chart.js library (CDN link)
// HTML structure for Chart.js Data Visualization
const chartContent = `
 <canvas id="myChart"></canvas>
`;
// Display Data Visualization chart
const chartContainer = document.createElement('div');
chartContainer.innerHTML = chartContent;
document.body.appendChild(chartContainer);
// Data for Chart.js
const labels = ['January', 'February', 'March', 'April', 'May'];
const data = {
 labels: labels,
 datasets: [{
  label: 'Sales Data',
  data: [65, 59, 80, 81, 56],
  backgroundColor: 'rgba(75, 192, 192, 0.2)',
  borderColor: 'rgba(75, 192, 192, 1)',
  borderWidth: 1
 }]
};

// Configuration options for Chart.js
const options = {
 scales: {
  y: {
   beginAtZero: true
  }
 }
```

```
};

// Create and display Chart.js chart
const ctx = document.getElementById('myChart').getContext('2d');
const myChart = new Chart(ctx, {
  type: 'bar',
  data: data,
  options: options
});
```

Implement Interactive Maps (using Leaflet.js)

```
// Sample implementation of Interactive Maps using Leaflet.js

// Include Leaflet.js library (CDN link)

// HTML structure for Leaflet.js Interactive Map
const mapContent = `
  <div id="map" style="height: 400px;"></div>
`;

// Display Interactive Map
const mapContainer = document.createElement('div');
mapContainer.innerHTML = mapContent;
document.body.appendChild(mapContainer);

// Initialize Leaflet.js map
const mymap = L.map('map').setView([51.505, -0.09], 13);

// Add Tile Layer (OpenStreetMap)
L.tileLayer('https://{s}.tile.openstreetmap.org/{z}/{x}/{y}.png', {
  maxZoom: 18,
```

```
  attribution: 'Map data © <a
href="https://www.openstreetmap.org/copyright">OpenStreetMap</a> contributors'
}).addTo(mymap);

// Add Marker to map
const marker = L.marker([51.5, -0.09]).addTo(mymap);
marker.bindPopup('Hello, World!').openPopup();
```

Implement Photo Editing Tool

```
// Sample implementation of a Photo Editing Tool (front-end only)

// HTML structure for Photo Editing Tool
const photoEditorContent = `
  <input type="file" accept="image/*">
  <canvas id="canvas"></canvas>
  <button onclick="applyFilter('grayscale')">Grayscale</button>
  <button onclick="applyFilter('sepia')">Sepia</button>
`;

// Display Photo Editing Tool
const photoEditorContainer = document.createElement('div');
photoEditorContainer.innerHTML = photoEditorContent;
document.body.appendChild(photoEditorContainer);

// Function to apply image filter
function applyFilter(filter) {
  const canvas = document.getElementById('canvas');
  const ctx = canvas.getContext('2d');
  const image = new Image();
  image.src = 'image.jpg';
  image.onload = () => {
```

```
    canvas.width = image.width;
    canvas.height = image.height;
    ctx.drawImage(image, 0, 0);
    if (filter === 'grayscale') {
      ctx.filter = 'grayscale(100%)';
    } else if (filter === 'sepia') {
      ctx.filter = 'sepia(100%)';
    }
    ctx.drawImage(image, 0, 0);
  };
}
```

Implement Drawing Board

```
// Sample implementation of a Drawing Board using Canvas
// HTML structure for Drawing Board
const drawingBoardContent = `
  <canvas id="drawingBoard" width="800" height="600"></canvas>
`;
// Display Drawing Board
const drawingBoardContainer = document.createElement('div');
drawingBoardContainer.innerHTML = drawingBoardContent;
document.body.appendChild(drawingBoardContainer);

// Initialize Drawing Board
const canvas = document.getElementById('drawingBoard');
const ctx = canvas.getContext('2d');
let isDrawing = false;
let lastX = 0;
let lastY = 0;

// Event listeners for Drawing Board
```

```
canvas.addEventListener('mousedown', startDrawing);
canvas.addEventListener('mousemove', draw);
canvas.addEventListener('mouseup', stopDrawing);
canvas.addEventListener('mouseout', stopDrawing);

// Drawing functions
function startDrawing(e) {
  isDrawing = true;
  [lastX, lastY] = [e.offsetX, e.offsetY];
}

function draw(e) {
  if (isDrawing) {
    ctx.beginPath();
    ctx.moveTo(lastX, lastY);
    ctx.lineTo(e.offsetX, e.offsetY);
    ctx.stroke();
    [lastX, lastY] = [e.offsetX, e.offsetY];
  }
}

function stopDrawing() {
  isDrawing = false;
}
```

Implement Video Chat Application

```
// Sample implementation of a Video Chat Application using WebRTC
// HTML structure for Video Chat Application
const videoChatContent = `
  <video id="localVideo" autoplay></video>
  <video id="remoteVideo" autoplay></video>
```

```
  <button onclick="startVideoChat()">Start Video Chat</button>
`;

// Display Video Chat Application
const videoChatContainer = document.createElement('div');
videoChatContainer.innerHTML = videoChatContent;
document.body.appendChild(videoChatContainer);

// Function to start video chat
async function startVideoChat() {
  const localStream = await navigator.mediaDevices.getUserMedia({ video: true, audio:
true });
  const localVideo = document.getElementById('localVideo');
  localVideo.srcObject = localStream;

  const peerConnection = new RTCPeerConnection();
  localStream.getTracks().forEach(track => peerConnection.addTrack(track,
localStream));

  peerConnection.ontrack = event => {
    const remoteVideo = document.getElementById('remoteVideo');
    remoteVideo.srcObject = event.streams[0];
  };

  const offer = await peerConnection.createOffer();
  await peerConnection.setLocalDescription(offer);

  // Send offer to remote peer (using signaling server)
}
```

Implement Task Scheduler

```
// Sample implementation of a Task Scheduler using localStorage
class TaskScheduler {
  constructor() {
    this.tasks = JSON.parse(localStorage.getItem('tasks')) || [];
  }
  addTask(task) {
    this.tasks.push(task);
    this.saveTasks();
  }

  deleteTask(index) {
    this.tasks.splice(index, 1);
    this.saveTasks();
  }
  saveTasks() {
    localStorage.setItem('tasks', JSON.stringify(this.tasks));
  }
  displayTasks() {
    console.log('--- Task List ---');
    this.tasks.forEach((task, index) => {
      console.log(`${index + 1}. ${task}`);
    });
    console.log('---');
  }
}
// Example usage of Task Scheduler
const taskScheduler = new TaskScheduler();
taskScheduler.addTask('Complete assignment');
taskScheduler.addTask('Prepare presentation');
taskScheduler.displayTasks();
```

```
taskScheduler.deleteTask(0);
taskScheduler.displayTasks();
```

Implement Expense Tracker

```
// Sample implementation of an Expense Tracker using localStorage
class ExpenseTracker {
 constructor() {
  this.expenses = JSON.parse(localStorage.getItem('expenses')) || [];
 }

 addExpense(item, amount) {
  this.expenses.push({ item, amount });
  this.saveExpenses();
 }

 deleteExpense(index) {
  this.expenses.splice(index, 1);
  this.saveExpenses();
 }

 saveExpenses() {
  localStorage.setItem('expenses', JSON.stringify(this.expenses));
 }

 displayExpenses() {
  console.log('--- Expenses ---');
  this.expenses.forEach((expense, index) => {
   console.log(`${index + 1}. ${expense.item}: $${expense.amount}`);
  });
  console.log('---');
 }
```

```
}

// Example usage of Expense Tracker
const expenseTracker = new ExpenseTracker();
expenseTracker.addExpense('Groceries', 50);
expenseTracker.addExpense('Shopping', 100);
expenseTracker.displayExpenses();
expenseTracker.deleteExpense(0);
expenseTracker.displayExpenses();
```

Implement RSS Feed Reader

```
// Sample implementation of an RSS Feed Reader using fetch API
// Function to fetch and display RSS feed
async function fetchRSSFeed(url) {
  try {
    const response = await fetch(url);
    const xmlText = await response.text();
    const parser = new DOMParser();
    const xml = parser.parseFromString(xmlText, 'text/xml');
    const items = xml.querySelectorAll('item');
    console.log('--- RSS Feed Items ---');
    items.forEach((item, index) => {
      const title = item.querySelector('title').textContent;
      console.log(`${index + 1}. ${title}`);
    });
    console.log('---');
  } catch (error) {
    console.error('Error fetching RSS feed:', error);
  }
}
```

```
// Example usage of RSS Feed Reader
const rssFeedUrl = 'https://example.com/feed';
fetchRSSFeed(rssFeedUrl);
```

Implement URL Shortener

```
// Sample implementation of a URL Shortener
class URLShortener {
  constructor() {
    this.urls = {};
    this.shortURLPrefix = 'https://short.url/';
  }

  shortenURL(longURL) {
    const shortCode = Math.random().toString(36).substr(2, 6);
    const shortURL = this.shortURLPrefix + shortCode;
    this.urls[shortCode] = longURL;
    return shortURL;
  }

  expandURL(shortURL) {
    const shortCode = shortURL.replace(this.shortURLPrefix, '');
    return this.urls[shortCode] || 'URL not found';
  }
}

// Example usage of URL Shortener
const urlShortener = new URLShortener();
const shortURL = urlShortener.shortenURL('https://example.com/very-long-url');
console.log('Short URL:', shortURL);
const originalURL = urlShortener.expandURL(shortURL);
console.log('Original URL:', originalURL);
```

Implement QR Code Generator

```
// Sample implementation of a QR Code Generator (using QRCode.js library)

// Include QRCode.js library (CDN link)

// Function to generate QR code
function generateQRCode(text) {
  const qrContainer = document.createElement('div');
  new QRCode(qrContainer, {
    text: text,
    width: 200,
    height: 200
  });
  return qrContainer;
}

// Example usage of QR Code Generator
const qrCodeElement = generateQRCode('https://example.com');
document.body.appendChild(qrCodeElement);
```

Implement Barcode Generator

```
// Sample implementation of a Barcode Generator (using JsBarcode library)

// Include JsBarcode library (CDN link)

// Function to generate barcode
function generateBarcode(text) {
  const barcodeImage = document.createElement('img');
  JsBarcode(barcodeImage, text, { format: 'CODE128' });
  return barcodeImage;
}
```

```
// Example usage of Barcode Generator
const barcodeElement = generateBarcode('123456789');
document.body.appendChild(barcodeElement);
```

Implement Password Manager

```
// Sample implementation of a Password Manager using localStorage

class PasswordManager {
  constructor() {
    this.passwords = JSON.parse(localStorage.getItem('passwords')) || {};
  }

  savePassword(username, password) {
    this.passwords[username] = password;
    this.savePasswords();
  }

  getPassword(username) {
    return this.passwords[username] || 'Password not found';
  }

  savePasswords() {
    localStorage.setItem('passwords', JSON.stringify(this.passwords));
  }
}

// Example usage of Password Manager
const passwordManager = new PasswordManager();
passwordManager.savePassword('user123', 'password123');
const retrievedPassword = passwordManager.getPassword('user123');
```

```
console.log('Retrieved Password:', retrievedPassword);
```

Implement Word Processor

```
// Sample implementation of a Word Processor using contenteditable

// HTML structure for Word Processor
const wordProcessorContent = `
  <div contenteditable="true" style="width: 100%; height: 300px; border: 1px solid
#ccc;"></div>
`;

// Display Word Processor
const wordProcessorContainer = document.createElement('div');
wordProcessorContainer.innerHTML = wordProcessorContent;
document.body.appendChild(wordProcessorContainer);
```

Implement Online Compiler

```
// Sample implementation of an Online Compiler (front-end only)
// HTML structure for Online Compiler
const onlineCompilerContent = `
  <textarea id="code" rows="10" cols="50">console.log('Hello, World!');</textarea>
  <button onclick="runCode()">Run Code</button>
  <div id="output"></div>
`;

// Display Online Compiler
const onlineCompilerContainer = document.createElement('div');
onlineCompilerContainer.innerHTML = onlineCompilerContent;
document.body.appendChild(onlineCompilerContainer);

// Function to run code
```

```
function runCode() {
  const code = document.getElementById('code').value;
  try {
    const result = eval(code);
    document.getElementById('output').textContent = String(result);
  } catch (error) {
    document.getElementById('output').textContent = 'Error: ' + error.message;
  }
}
```

Implement Markdown Previewer

```
// Sample implementation of a Markdown Previewer

// Include marked.js library (CDN link)

// HTML structure for Markdown Previewer
const markdownPreviewerContent = `
  <textarea id="markdownInput" rows="10" cols="50"># Markdown
Previewer\n\n**Markdown** is supported!\n\n- List item 1\n- List item
2\n\n[Link](https://example.com)\n\n\`\`\`javascript\nconsole.log('Hello,
World!');\n\`\`\`\n`;

// Display Markdown Previewer
const markdownPreviewerContainer = document.createElement('div');
markdownPreviewerContainer.innerHTML = markdownPreviewerContent;
document.body.appendChild(markdownPreviewerContainer);

// Event listener for markdown input
const markdownInput = document.getElementById('markdownInput');
markdownInput.addEventListener('input', () => {
  const markdownContent = markdownInput.value;
```

```
  const markdownHtml = marked(markdownContent);
  const previewElement = document.createElement('div');
  previewElement.innerHTML = markdownHtml;
  document.body.appendChild(previewElement);
});
```

Implement 3D Graphics (using Three.js)

```
// Sample implementation of 3D Graphics using Three.js
// Include Three.js library (CDN link)

// Initialize Three.js scene
const scene = new THREE.Scene();
const camera = new THREE.PerspectiveCamera(75, window.innerWidth /
window.innerHeight, 0.1, 1000);
const renderer = new THREE.WebGLRenderer();
renderer.setSize(window.innerWidth, window.innerHeight);
document.body.appendChild(renderer.domElement);

// Create a cube
const geometry = new THREE.BoxGeometry();
const material = new THREE.MeshBasicMaterial({ color: 0x00ff00 });
const cube = new THREE.Mesh(geometry, material);
scene.add(cube);

// Position the camera
camera.position.z = 5;

// Render loop
const animate = function () {
  requestAnimationFrame(animate);
  cube.rotation.x += 0.01;
```

```
  cube.rotation.y += 0.01;
  renderer.render(scene, camera);
};

animate();
```

Implement WebGL Applications

```
// Sample implementation of WebGL Applications using WebGL API

// Initialize WebGL context
const canvas = document.createElement('canvas');
canvas.width = window.innerWidth;
canvas.height = window.innerHeight;
document.body.appendChild(canvas);

const gl = canvas.getContext('webgl');

if (!gl) {
  console.error('WebGL not supported');
} else {
  gl.clearColor(0.0, 0.0, 0.0, 1.0);
  gl.clear(gl.COLOR_BUFFER_BIT);
}
```

Implement Voice Recognition

```
// Sample implementation of Voice Recognition using Web Speech API
// Initialize SpeechRecognition object
const recognition = new webkitSpeechRecognition(); // for Chrome
recognition.continuous = true;
recognition.lang = 'en-US';
```

```
// Event listener for speech recognition
recognition.onresult = function(event) {
  const transcript = event.results[event.results.length - 1][0].transcript;
  console.log('Speech recognized:', transcript);
};

// Start speech recognition
recognition.start();
```

Implement Speech Synthesis

```
// Sample implementation of Speech Synthesis using Web Speech API
// Function to speak text
function speak(text) {
  const utterance = new SpeechSynthesisUtterance(text);
  window.speechSynthesis.speak(utterance);
}

// Example usage of Speech Synthesis
speak('Hello, welcome to the speech synthesis demonstration.');
```

Implement Virtual Keyboard

```
// Sample implementation of Virtual Keyboard
// HTML structure for Virtual Keyboard
const virtualKeyboardContent = `
  <input type="text" id="textInput">
  <div id="virtualKeyboard">
    <button onclick="typeCharacter('A')">A</button>
    <button onclick="typeCharacter('B')">B</button>
    <!-- Add more buttons for other characters -->
  </div>
`;
```

```
// Display Virtual Keyboard
const virtualKeyboardContainer = document.createElement('div');
virtualKeyboardContainer.innerHTML = virtualKeyboardContent;
document.body.appendChild(virtualKeyboardContainer);

// Function to type character
function typeCharacter(char) {
  const textInput = document.getElementById('textInput');
  textInput.value += char;
}
```

Implement Virtual Assistant

```
// Sample implementation of Virtual Assistant
// Function to process user input and provide responses
function virtualAssistant(input) {
  if (input.includes('hello')) {
    return 'Hello! How can I assist you today?';
  } else if (input.includes('weather')) {
    return 'The weather is currently sunny.';
  } else {
    return 'I'm sorry, I didn't understand that.';
  }
}

// Example usage of Virtual Assistant
const userInput = 'What is the weather like?';
const response = virtualAssistant(userInput);
console.log('Virtual Assistant:', response);
```

Implement AI Chatbot

```
// Sample implementation of AI Chatbot using TensorFlow.js and a pre-trained model
// Load pre-trained model (example)
const model = await tf.loadLayersModel('https://example.com/chatbot-
model/model.json');
// Function to generate response from chatbot
function chatbot(input) {
  const encodedInput = preprocessInput(input);
  const prediction = model.predict(encodedInput);
  const response = decodeOutput(prediction);
  return response;
}

// Example usage of AI Chatbot
const userInput = 'How can I track my order?';
const botResponse = chatbot(userInput);
console.log('Chatbot Response:', botResponse);
```

Implement Machine Learning Models (using TensorFlow.js)

```
// Sample implementation of Machine Learning Models using TensorFlow.js
// Load pre-trained model (example)
const model = await tf.loadLayersModel('https://example.com/machine-learning-
model/model.json');

// Function to make predictions using the model
function predict(inputData) {
  const inputTensor = tf.tensor(inputData);
  const prediction = model.predict(inputTensor);
  return prediction.dataSync();
}
```

```
// Example usage of Machine Learning Model
const inputData = [1, 2, 3, 4];
const predictionResult = predict(inputData);
console.log('Prediction Result:', predictionResult);
```

Implement Browser Extensions

```
// Sample implementation of a Browser Extension (Chrome extension)
// Manifest file (manifest.json) for Chrome extension
{
  "manifest_version": 2,
  "name": "My Extension",
  "version": "1.0",
  "permissions": ["activeTab"],
  "content_scripts": [{
    "matches": ["<all_urls>"],
    "js": ["contentScript.js"]
  }],
  "browser_action": {
    "default_popup": "popup.html"
  }
}

// Content script (contentScript.js) for Chrome extension
console.log('Content script loaded.');

// Popup HTML (popup.html) for Chrome extension
<!DOCTYPE html>
<html>
<head>
  <title>Extension Popup</title>
</head>
```

```
<body>
  <h1>Hello, this is my extension!</h1>
</body>
</html>
```

Implement Web Scraping Tool

```
// Sample implementation of a Web Scraping Tool using Puppeteer (headless Chrome)
const puppeteer = require('puppeteer');

(async () => {
  const browser = await puppeteer.launch();
  const page = await browser.newPage();
  await page.goto('https://example.com');

  const pageTitle = await page.title();
  console.log('Page Title:', pageTitle);

  const pageContent = await page.content();
  console.log('Page Content:', pageContent);

  await browser.close();
})();
```

Implement Email Client

```
// Sample implementation of an Email Client using IMAP.js (IMAP client library)
const Imap = require('imap');
const simpleParser = require('mailparser').simpleParser;

const imap = new Imap({
  user: 'your_email@example.com',
  password: 'your_password',
```

```
  host: 'imap.example.com',
  port: 993,
  tls: true
});

imap.connect();

imap.on('ready', () => {
  imap.openBox('INBOX', false, (err, box) => {
    if (err) throw err;
    imap.search(['UNSEEN'], (err, results) => {
      if (err) throw err;
      results.forEach(uid => {
        const f = imap.fetch(uid, { bodies: '' });
        f.on('message', (msg) => {
          simpleParser(msg, (err, parsed) => {
            if (err) throw err;
            console.log('New Email:', parsed.subject);
          });
        });
      });
    });
  });
});

imap.on('error', (err) => {
  console.error('IMAP error:', err);
});
```

Implement Music Playlist App

```
// Sample implementation of a Music Playlist App
// Define MusicPlaylist class
class MusicPlaylist {
  constructor() {
    this.playlist = [];
    this.currentTrackIndex = 0;
  }

  addTrack(track) {
    this.playlist.push(track);
  }

  playNextTrack() {
    if (this.currentTrackIndex < this.playlist.length) {
      const currentTrack = this.playlist[this.currentTrackIndex];
      console.log('Now playing:', currentTrack);
      this.currentTrackIndex++;
    } else {
      console.log('End of playlist.');
    }
  }
}

// Example usage of Music Playlist App
const myPlaylist = new MusicPlaylist();
myPlaylist.addTrack('Track 1');
myPlaylist.addTrack('Track 2');
myPlaylist.addTrack('Track 3');
myPlaylist.playNextTrack();
myPlaylist.playNextTrack();
```

```
myPlaylist.playNextTrack();
myPlaylist.playNextTrack();
```

Implement Recipe Finder

```
// Sample implementation of a Recipe Finder using Spoonacular API

// Function to search for recipes
async function searchRecipes(query) {
  const apiKey = 'your_api_key';
  const response = await
fetch(`https://api.spoonacular.com/recipes/search?query=${query}&apiKey=${apiKey}`
);
  const data = await response.json();
  return data.results;
}

// Example usage of Recipe Finder
const recipes = await searchRecipes('pasta');
console.log('Recipes:', recipes);
```

Implement Expense Sharing App

```
// Sample implementation of an Expense Sharing App using localStorage
class ExpenseSharingApp {
  constructor() {
    this.expenses = JSON.parse(localStorage.getItem('expenses')) || [];
  }

  addExpense(description, amount) {
    this.expenses.push({ description, amount });
    this.saveExpenses();
  }
```

```
  getTotalExpenses() {
    return this.expenses.reduce((total, expense) => total + expense.amount, 0);
  }

  saveExpenses() {
    localStorage.setItem('expenses', JSON.stringify(this.expenses));
  }
}

// Example usage of Expense Sharing App
const expenseApp = new ExpenseSharingApp();
expenseApp.addExpense('Dinner', 50);
expenseApp.addExpense('Shopping', 100);
const totalExpenses = expenseApp.getTotalExpenses();
console.log('Total Expenses:', totalExpenses);
```

Implement Weather Forecast Widget

```
// Sample implementation of a Weather Forecast Widget using OpenWeatherMap API
// Function to fetch weather forecast data
async function fetchWeatherForecast(city) {
  const apiKey = 'your_api_key';
  const response = await
fetch(`https://api.openweathermap.org/data/2.5/weather?q=${city}&appid=${apiKey}`);
  const data = await response.json();
  return data;
}

// Example usage of Weather Forecast Widget
const city = 'New York';
fetchWeatherForecast(city)
```

```
  .then(data => {
    console.log('Weather Forecast for', city + ':', data);
  })
  .catch(error => {
    console.error('Error fetching weather forecast:', error);
  });
```

Implement News Aggregator

```
// Sample implementation of a News Aggregator using News API
// Function to fetch top headlines
async function fetchTopHeadlines(countryCode) {
  const apiKey = 'your_api_key';
  const response = await fetch(`https://newsapi.org/v2/top-
headlines?country=${countryCode}&apiKey=${apiKey}`);
  const data = await response.json();
  return data.articles;
}
// Example usage of News Aggregator
const countryCode = 'us';
fetchTopHeadlines(countryCode)
  .then(articles => {
    console.log('Top Headlines (US):', articles);
  })
  .catch(error => {
    console.error('Error fetching top headlines:', error);
  });
```

Implement Cryptocurrency Tracker

```
// Sample implementation of a Cryptocurrency Tracker using CoinGecko API
// Function to fetch cryptocurrency data
async function fetchCryptoData() {
```

```
  const response = await
fetch('https://api.coingecko.com/api/v3/coins/markets?vs_currency=usd&ids=bitcoin,eth
ereum,litecoin');
  const data = await response.json();
  return data;
}

// Example usage of Cryptocurrency Tracker
fetchCryptoData()
  .then(coins => {
    console.log('Cryptocurrencies:', coins);
  })
  .catch(error => {
    console.error('Error fetching cryptocurrency data:', error);
  });
```

Implement Stock Market Tracker

```
// Sample implementation of a Stock Market Tracker using Alpha Vantage API
// Function to fetch stock market data
async function fetchStockData(symbol) {
  const apiKey = 'your_api_key';
  const response = await
fetch(`https://www.alphavantage.co/query?function=TIME_SERIES_DAILY&symbol=
${symbol}&apikey=${apiKey}`);
  const data = await response.json();
  return data['Time Series (Daily)'];
}
// Example usage of Stock Market Tracker
const stockSymbol = 'AAPL';
fetchStockData(stockSymbol)
  .then(dailyData => {
```

```
    console.log('Stock Data (AAPL):', dailyData);
  })
  .catch(error => {
    console.error('Error fetching stock data:', error);
  });
```

Implement Flight Booking System

```
// Sample implementation of a Flight Booking System using Amadeus API
// Function to search for flights
async function searchFlights(origin, destination, departureDate, adults) {
  const apiKey = 'your_api_key';
  const response = await fetch(`https://test.api.amadeus.com/v2/shopping/flight-offers?originLocationCode=${origin}&destinationLocationCode=${destination}&departureDate=${departureDate}&adults=${adults}&currencyCode=USD&nonStop=true&max=5`, {
    headers: {
      'Authorization': `Bearer ${apiKey}`
    }
  });
  const data = await response.json();
  return data.data;
}

// Example usage of Flight Booking System
const flightOptions = {
  origin: 'JFK',
  destination: 'LAX',
  departureDate: '2024-05-01',
  adults: 1
};
```

```
searchFlights(flightOptions.origin, flightOptions.destination,
flightOptions.departureDate, flightOptions.adults)
  .then(flights => {
    console.log('Flight Options:', flights);
  })
  .catch(error => {
    console.error('Error searching flights:', error);
  });
```

Implement Hotel Booking System

```
// Sample implementation of a Hotel Booking System using Booking.com API
// Function to search for hotels
async function searchHotels(city, checkInDate, checkOutDate, guests) {
  const apiKey = 'your_api_key';
  const response = await
fetch(`https://hotels4.p.rapidapi.com/locations/search?query=${city}&locale=en_US`, {
    headers: {
      'x-rapidapi-key': apiKey
    }
  });
  const locationData = await response.json();
  const locationId = locationData.suggestions[0].entities[0].destinationId;

  const hotelResponse = await
fetch(`https://hotels4.p.rapidapi.com/properties/list?destinationId=${locationId}&pageN
umber=1&checkIn=${checkInDate}&checkOut=${checkOutDate}&pageSize=5&adults
1=${guests}&currency=USD&locale=en_US&sortOrder=PRICE`, {
    headers: {
      'x-rapidapi-key': apiKey
    }
  });
```

```
  const hotelData = await hotelResponse.json();
  return hotelData.data.body.searchResults.results;
}

// Example usage of Hotel Booking System
const hotelOptions = {
  city: 'New York',
  checkInDate: '2024-06-01',
  checkOutDate: '2024-06-05',
  guests: 2
};

searchHotels(hotelOptions.city, hotelOptions.checkInDate, hotelOptions.checkOutDate,
hotelOptions.guests)
  .then(hotels => {
    console.log('Hotel Options:', hotels);
  })
  .catch(error => {
    console.error('Error searching hotels:', error);
  });
```

Implement Online Banking System

```
// Sample implementation of an Online Banking System using localStorage
class OnlineBankingSystem {
  constructor() {
    this.accounts = JSON.parse(localStorage.getItem('accounts')) || {};
  }

  createAccount(username, password, initialBalance) {
    this.accounts[username] = {
      password,
```

```
      balance: initialBalance
    };
    this.saveAccounts();
  }

  deposit(username, amount) {
    if (this.accounts[username]) {
      this.accounts[username].balance += amount;
      this.saveAccounts();
    } else {
      console.error('Account not found');
    }
  }

  withdraw(username, amount) {
    if (this.accounts[username]) {
      if (this.accounts[username].balance >= amount) {
        this.accounts[username].balance -= amount;
        this.saveAccounts();
      } else {
        console.error('Insufficient balance');
      }
    } else {
      console.error('Account not found');
    }
  }

  saveAccounts() {
    localStorage.setItem('accounts', JSON.stringify(this.accounts));
  }
}
```

```
// Example usage of Online Banking System
const bankingSystem = new OnlineBankingSystem();
bankingSystem.createAccount('user123', 'password123', 1000);
bankingSystem.deposit('user123', 500);
bankingSystem.withdraw('user123', 200);
console.log('Account Details:', bankingSystem.accounts['user123']);
```

Implement Healthcare Management System

```
// Sample implementation of a Healthcare Management System using localStorage
class HealthcareManagementSystem {
  constructor() {
    this.patients = JSON.parse(localStorage.getItem('patients')) || [];
  }

  addPatient(name, age, condition) {
    this.patients.push({ name, age, condition });
    this.savePatients();
  }

  removePatient(index) {
    this.patients.splice(index, 1);
    this.savePatients();
  }

  savePatients() {
    localStorage.setItem('patients', JSON.stringify(this.patients));
  }
}

// Example usage of Healthcare Management System
```

```
const healthcareSystem = new HealthcareManagementSystem();
healthcareSystem.addPatient('John Doe', 30, 'Fever');
healthcareSystem.addPatient('Jane Doe', 25, 'Cough');
healthcareSystem.removePatient(0);
console.log('Patients:', healthcareSystem.patients);
```

Implement Inventory Management System

```
// Sample implementation of an Inventory Management System using localStorage
class InventoryManagementSystem {
  constructor() {
    this.inventory = JSON.parse(localStorage.getItem('inventory')) || {};
  }
  addItem(itemName, quantity) {
    if (this.inventory[itemName]) {
      this.inventory[itemName] += quantity;
    } else {
      this.inventory[itemName] = quantity;
    }
    this.saveInventory();
  }

  removeItem(itemName, quantity) {
    if (this.inventory[itemName]) {
      if (this.inventory[itemName] >= quantity) {
        this.inventory[itemName] -= quantity;
        if (this.inventory[itemName] === 0) {
          delete this.inventory[itemName];
        }
        this.saveInventory();
      } else {
        console.error('Insufficient quantity');
```

```
    }
   } else {
    console.error('Item not found');
   }
  }

  saveInventory() {
   localStorage.setItem('inventory', JSON.stringify(this.inventory));
  }
}

// Example usage of Inventory Management System
const inventorySystem = new InventoryManagementSystem();
inventorySystem.addItem('Laptop', 10);
inventorySystem.addItem('Mouse', 20);
inventorySystem.removeItem('Laptop', 5);
console.log('Inventory:', inventorySystem.inventory);
```

Implement Student Management System

```
// Sample implementation of a Student Management System using localStorage
class StudentManagementSystem {
  constructor() {
   this.students = JSON.parse(localStorage.getItem('students')) || [];
  }

  addStudent(name, grade, age) {
   this.students.push({ name, grade, age });
   this.saveStudents();
  }

  removeStudent(index) {
```

```
    this.students.splice(index, 1);
    this.saveStudents();
  }

  saveStudents() {
    localStorage.setItem('students', JSON.stringify(this.students));
  }
}

// Example usage of Student Management System
const studentSystem = new StudentManagementSystem();
studentSystem.addStudent('John Doe', 'A', 15);
studentSystem.addStudent('Jane Doe', 'B', 14);
studentSystem.removeStudent(0);
console.log('Students:', studentSystem.students);
```

Implement Library Management System

```
// Sample implementation of a Library Management System using localStorage
class LibraryManagementSystem {
  constructor() {
    this.books = JSON.parse(localStorage.getItem('books')) || [];
  }

  addBook(title, author, isbn) {
    this.books.push({ title, author, isbn });
    this.saveBooks();
  }

  removeBook(index) {
    this.books.splice(index, 1);
    this.saveBooks();
```

```
  }
  saveBooks() {
    localStorage.setItem('books', JSON.stringify(this.books));
  }
}

// Example usage of Library Management System
const librarySystem = new LibraryManagementSystem();
librarySystem.addBook('JavaScript: The Good Parts', 'Douglas Crockford',
'9780596517748');
librarySystem.addBook('Clean Code', 'Robert C. Martin', '9780132350884');
librarySystem.removeBook(0);
console.log('Books:', librarySystem.books);
```

Implement Ticket Booking System

```
// Sample implementation of a Ticket Booking System
class TicketBookingSystem {
  constructor() {
    this.bookedTickets = [];
  }

  bookTicket(user, event, quantity) {
    const ticket = { user, event, quantity };
    this.bookedTickets.push(ticket);
    console.log(`Ticket booked successfully for ${user} - ${event} (${quantity}
tickets)`);
  }

  cancelTicket(user, event) {
    const index = this.bookedTickets.findIndex(ticket => ticket.user === user &&
ticket.event === event);
```

```
    if (index !== -1) {
      this.bookedTickets.splice(index, 1);
      console.log(`Ticket cancelled successfully for ${user} - ${event}`);
    } else {
      console.log(`No ticket found for ${user} - ${event}`);
    }
  }

  displayBookedTickets() {
    console.log('Booked Tickets:', this.bookedTickets);
  }
}

// Example usage of Ticket Booking System
const ticketSystem = new TicketBookingSystem();
ticketSystem.bookTicket('John Doe', 'Concert', 2);
ticketSystem.bookTicket('Jane Doe', 'Movie', 3);
ticketSystem.displayBookedTickets();
ticketSystem.cancelTicket('John Doe', 'Concert');
ticketSystem.displayBookedTickets();
```

Implement Food Delivery App

```
// Sample implementation of a Food Delivery App
class FoodDeliveryApp {
  constructor() {
    this.orders = [];
  }

  placeOrder(customerName, items, totalPrice) {
    const order = { customerName, items, totalPrice };
    this.orders.push(order);
```

```
    console.log(`Order placed successfully for ${customerName}:`, items);
  }

  cancelOrder(customerName) {
    const index = this.orders.findIndex(order => order.customerName ===
customerName);
    if (index !== -1) {
      this.orders.splice(index, 1);
      console.log(`Order cancelled successfully for ${customerName}`);
    } else {
      console.log(`No order found for ${customerName}`);
    }
  }

  displayOrders() {
    console.log('Orders:', this.orders);
  }
}

// Example usage of Food Delivery App
const foodApp = new FoodDeliveryApp();
foodApp.placeOrder('John Doe', ['Pizza', 'Burger', 'Salad'], 30);
foodApp.placeOrder('Jane Doe', ['Sushi', 'Ramen'], 25);
foodApp.displayOrders();
foodApp.cancelOrder('John Doe');
foodApp.displayOrders();
```

Implement Ride Sharing App

```
// Sample implementation of a Ride Sharing App
class RideSharingApp {
  constructor() {
```

```
    this.rides = [];
  }

  offerRide(driver, origin, destination, seatsAvailable) {
    const ride = { driver, origin, destination, seatsAvailable };
    this.rides.push(ride);
    console.log(`Ride offered successfully by ${driver} from ${origin} to
${destination}`);
  }

  bookRide(passenger, origin, destination) {
    const ride = this.rides.find(ride => ride.origin === origin && ride.destination ===
destination && ride.seatsAvailable > 0);
    if (ride) {
      ride.seatsAvailable--;
      console.log(`Ride booked successfully for ${passenger} from ${origin} to
${destination}`);
    } else {
      console.log(`No available ride found from ${origin} to ${destination}`);
    }
  }

  displayAvailableRides() {
    console.log('Available Rides:', this.rides);
  }
}

// Example usage of Ride Sharing App
const rideApp = new RideSharingApp();
rideApp.offerRide('John', 'City A', 'City B', 3);
rideApp.offerRide('Jane', 'City B', 'City C', 2);
```

```
rideApp.displayAvailableRides();
rideApp.bookRide('Alice', 'City A', 'City B');
rideApp.displayAvailableRides();
```

Implement Fitness Tracker

```
// Sample implementation of a Fitness Tracker
class FitnessTracker {
  constructor() {
    this.activities = [];
  }

  trackActivity(activity, duration) {
    const record = { activity, duration };
    this.activities.push(record);
    console.log(`Activity "${activity}" tracked successfully for ${duration} minutes`);
  }

  getTotalDuration() {
    const totalDuration = this.activities.reduce((total, record) => total + record.duration,
0);
    console.log('Total Activity Duration:', totalDuration, 'minutes');
  }

  displayActivities() {
    console.log('Tracked Activities:', this.activities);
  }
}

// Example usage of Fitness Tracker
const fitnessTracker = new FitnessTracker();
fitnessTracker.trackActivity('Running', 30);
```

```
fitnessTracker.trackActivity('Cycling', 45);
fitnessTracker.displayActivities();
fitnessTracker.getTotalDuration();
```

Implement Job Portal

```
// Sample implementation of a Job Portal
class JobPortal {
  constructor() {
    this.jobListings = [];
  }

  postJob(jobTitle, company, location, salary) {
    const jobListing = { jobTitle, company, location, salary };
    this.jobListings.push(jobListing);
    console.log(`Job "${jobTitle}" posted successfully at ${company} (${location}) -
Salary: ${salary}`);
  }

  searchJobs(keyword) {
    const matchedJobs = this.jobListings.filter(job =>
job.jobTitle.toLowerCase().includes(keyword.toLowerCase()));
    console.log('Matching Jobs:', matchedJobs);
  }

  displayJobListings() {
    console.log('Job Listings:', this.jobListings);
  }
}

// Example usage of Job Portal
const jobPortal = new JobPortal();
```

```
jobPortal.postJob('Web Developer', 'ABC Inc.', 'New York', '$80,000');
jobPortal.postJob('Software Engineer', 'XYZ Corp.', 'San Francisco', '$100,000');
jobPortal.displayJobListings();
jobPortal.searchJobs('developer');
```

Implement Dating App

```
// Sample implementation of a Dating App
class DatingApp {
  constructor() {
    this.profiles = [];
  }

  createProfile(name, age, gender, interests) {
    const profile = { name, age, gender, interests };
    this.profiles.push(profile);
    console.log(`Profile created successfully for ${name} - Age: ${age}, Gender:
${gender}`);
  }

  matchProfiles(interests) {
    const matchedProfiles = this.profiles.filter(profile =>
profile.interests.includes(interests));
    console.log('Matching Profiles:', matchedProfiles);
  }

  displayProfiles() {
    console.log('User Profiles:', this.profiles);
  }
}

// Example usage of Dating App
```

```
const datingApp = new DatingApp();
datingApp.createProfile('John Doe', 30, 'Male', ['Reading', 'Traveling', 'Music']);
datingApp.createProfile('Jane Doe', 28, 'Female', ['Cooking', 'Movies', 'Photography']);
datingApp.displayProfiles();
datingApp.matchProfiles('Traveling');
```

Implement Social Networking Site

```
// Sample implementation of a Social Networking Site
class SocialNetworkingSite {
 constructor() {
  this.users = [];
 }
 createUser(username, email, bio) {
  const user = { username, email, bio };
  this.users.push(user);
  console.log(`User ${username} created successfully`);
 }

 deleteUser(username) {
  const index = this.users.findIndex(user => user.username === username);
  if (index !== -1) {
   this.users.splice(index, 1);
   console.log(`User ${username} deleted successfully`);
  } else {
   console.log(`User ${username} not found`);
  }
 }

 displayUsers() {
  console.log('Users:', this.users);
 }
```

```
}

// Example usage of Social Networking Site
const socialNetworkingSite = new SocialNetworkingSite();
socialNetworkingSite.createUser('JohnDoe', 'john@example.com', 'Hello! I am John');
socialNetworkingSite.createUser('JaneDoe', 'jane@example.com', 'Nice to meet you!');
socialNetworkingSite.displayUsers();
socialNetworkingSite.deleteUser('JohnDoe');
socialNetworkingSite.displayUsers();
```

Implement Auction System

```
// Sample implementation of an Auction System

class AuctionSystem {
  constructor() {
    this.auctions = [];
  }

  createAuction(itemName, startingPrice, endDate) {
    const auction = { itemName, startingPrice, endDate };
    this.auctions.push(auction);
    console.log(`Auction created for ${itemName} - Starting Price: ${startingPrice}, End
Date: ${endDate}`);
  }

  placeBid(itemName, bidderName, bidAmount) {
    const auction = this.auctions.find(auction => auction.itemName === itemName &&
auction.endDate > new Date());
    if (auction) {
      console.log(`Bid placed by ${bidderName} for ${itemName} - Amount:
${bidAmount}`);
```

```
    } else {
      console.log(`Auction not found or expired for ${itemName}`);
    }
  }

  displayAuctions() {
    console.log('Active Auctions:', this.auctions.filter(auction => auction.endDate > new
Date()));
  }
}

// Example usage of Auction System
const auctionSystem = new AuctionSystem();
auctionSystem.createAuction('Painting', '$500', new Date('2024-06-30'));
auctionSystem.createAuction('Antique Watch', '$1000', new Date('2024-07-15'));
auctionSystem.displayAuctions();
auctionSystem.placeBid('Painting', 'JohnDoe', '$600');
auctionSystem.displayAuctions();
```

Implement Online Gaming Platform

```
// Sample implementation of an Online Gaming Platform
class OnlineGamingPlatform {
  constructor() {
    this.games = [];
  }

  addGame(gameTitle, genre, rating) {
    const game = { gameTitle, genre, rating };
    this.games.push(game);
    console.log(`Game "${gameTitle}" added successfully - Genre: ${genre}, Rating:
${rating}`);
```

```
  }

  removeGame(gameTitle) {
    const index = this.games.findIndex(game => game.gameTitle === gameTitle);
    if (index !== -1) {
      this.games.splice(index, 1);
      console.log(`Game "${gameTitle}" removed successfully`);
    } else {
      console.log(`Game "${gameTitle}" not found`);
    }
  }

  displayGames() {
    console.log('Available Games:', this.games);
  }
}

// Example usage of Online Gaming Platform
const gamingPlatform = new OnlineGamingPlatform();
gamingPlatform.addGame('Fortnite', 'Battle Royale', '4.5/5');
gamingPlatform.addGame('Minecraft', 'Adventure', '4.8/5');
gamingPlatform.displayGames();
gamingPlatform.removeGame('Fortnite');
gamingPlatform.displayGames();
```

Implement Multiplayer Game

```
// Sample implementation of a Multiplayer Game
class MultiplayerGame {
  constructor() {
    this.players = [];
  }
```

```
  addPlayer(playerName) {
    this.players.push(playerName);
    console.log(`Player ${playerName} joined the game`);
  }

  removePlayer(playerName) {
    const index = this.players.indexOf(playerName);
    if (index !== -1) {
      this.players.splice(index, 1);
      console.log(`Player ${playerName} left the game`);
    } else {
      console.log(`Player ${playerName} not found in the game`);
    }
  }

  displayPlayers() {
    console.log('Current Players:', this.players);
  }
}

// Example usage of Multiplayer Game
const multiplayerGame = new MultiplayerGame();
multiplayerGame.addPlayer('Player1');
multiplayerGame.addPlayer('Player2');
multiplayerGame.displayPlayers();
multiplayerGame.removePlayer('Player1');
multiplayerGame.displayPlayers();
```

Implement Virtual Reality (VR) Experience

```
// Sample implementation of a Virtual Reality (VR) Experience using A-Frame
// HTML:
/*
<!DOCTYPE html>
<html>
<head>
  <script src="https://aframe.io/releases/1.2.0/aframe.min.js"></script>
</head>
<body>
  <a-scene>
    <a-sky src="background.jpg" rotation="0 -90 0"></a-sky>
    <a-box position="-1 0.5 -3" rotation="0 45 0" color="#4CC3D9"></a-box>
    <a-sphere position="0 1.25 -5" radius="1.25" color="#EF2D5E"></a-sphere>
    <a-cylinder position="1 0.75 -3" radius="0.5" height="1.5" color="#FFC65D"></a-
cylinder>
    <a-plane position="0 0 -4" rotation="-90 0 0" width="4" height="4"
color="#7BC8A4"></a-plane>
  </a-scene>
</body>
</html>
*/
```

Implement Augmented Reality (AR) App

```
// Sample implementation of an Augmented Reality (AR) App using AR.js

// HTML:
/*
<!DOCTYPE html>
<html>
<head>
```

```
  <script src="https://aframe.io/releases/1.2.0/aframe.min.js"></script>
  <script src="https://raw.githack.com/AR-js-org/AR.js/master/aframe/build/aframe-ar-nft.js"></script>
</head>
<body style="margin: 0; overflow: hidden;">
  <a-scene embedded arjs>
    <a-nft
      type="nft"
      url="path/to/your/nft-image"
      smooth="true"
      smoothCount="10"
      smoothTolerance=".01"
      smoothThreshold="5"
    >
      <a-box position="0 0.5 0" material="color: yellow;"></a-box>
    </a-nft>
    <a-marker-camera preset="hiro"></a-marker-camera>
  </a-scene>
</body>
</html>
*/
```

Implement IoT Applications

```
// Sample implementation of an IoT Application using Node.js and MQTT
// Node.js Server:
const mqtt = require('mqtt');
const client = mqtt.connect('mqtt://broker.hivemq.com');

client.on('connect', () => {
  console.log('Connected to MQTT Broker');
```

```
  // Subscribe to IoT topic
  client.subscribe('iot/devices');

  // Publish data to IoT topic
  setInterval(() => {
    const temperature = Math.floor(Math.random() * 50) + 20;
    client.publish('iot/devices', `Temperature: ${temperature}°C`);
  }, 5000);
});

client.on('message', (topic, message) => {
  console.log(`Received message on topic ${topic}: ${message.toString()}`);
});
```

Implement Smart Home Automation

```
// Sample implementation of a Smart Home Automation system using JavaScript
class SmartHomeAutomation {
  constructor() {
    this.devices = {};
  }

  addDevice(deviceName, status) {
    this.devices[deviceName] = status;
    console.log(`Added ${deviceName} to Smart Home - Status: ${status}`);
  }

  toggleDevice(deviceName) {
    if (this.devices[deviceName]) {
      this.devices[deviceName] = !this.devices[deviceName];
      console.log(`${deviceName} toggled - New Status: ${this.devices[deviceName]}`);
    } else {
```

```
      console.log(`Device ${deviceName} not found`);
    }
  }

  displayDevices() {
    console.log('Smart Home Devices:', this.devices);
  }
}

// Example usage of Smart Home Automation
const smartHome = new SmartHomeAutomation();
smartHome.addDevice('Light Bulb', false);
smartHome.addDevice('Thermostat', true);
smartHome.toggleDevice('Light Bulb');
smartHome.displayDevices();
```

Implement Robotics Control System

```
// Sample implementation of a Robotics Control System using JavaScript and Arduino
// Arduino Code (C/C++):
/*
#include <Servo.h>
Servo motor;

void setup() {
  motor.attach(9); // Attach servo to pin 9
}

void loop() {
  motor.write(90); // Rotate servo to 90 degrees
  delay(1000);
  motor.write(0); // Rotate servo to 0 degrees
```

```
 delay(1000);
}
*/
```

Implement Drone Control System

```
// Sample implementation of a Drone Control System using JavaScript and Node.js

const Drone = require('drone-api');

const drone = new Drone();

drone.connect('your_drone_ip_address', 8888)
 .then(() => {
  console.log('Drone connected');
  drone.takeOff();

  setTimeout(() => {
   drone.land();
  }, 5000);
 })
 .catch(error => {
  console.error('Error connecting to drone:', error);
 });
```

Implement Gesture Recognition System

```
// Sample implementation of a Gesture Recognition System using TensorFlow.js
// HTML:
/*
<!DOCTYPE html>
<html>
<head>
```

```
  <script src="https://cdn.jsdelivr.net/npm/@tensorflow/tfjs"></script>
  <script src="https://cdn.jsdelivr.net/npm/@tensorflow-models/handpose"></script>
</head>
<body>
  <video id="video" width="640" height="480" autoplay></video>
  <canvas id="canvas" width="640" height="480"></canvas>
  <script>
    navigator.mediaDevices.getUserMedia({ video: true })
      .then(stream => {
        const video = document.getElementById('video');
        video.srcObject = stream;
        video.onloadedmetadata = () => {
          video.play();
          const canvas = document.getElementById('canvas');
          const context = canvas.getContext('2d');
          const handpose = require('@tensorflow-models/handpose');
          handpose.load()
            .then(model => {
              setInterval(() => {
                detectGesture(video, model, context);
              }, 100);
            });
        };
      });
    function detectGesture(video, model, context) {
      model.estimateHands(video)
        .then(predictions => {
          if (predictions.length > 0) {
            const keypoints = predictions[0].landmarks;
            // Implement gesture recognition logic here
            console.log('Hand keypoints:', keypoints);
```

```
        }
      });
    }
  </script>
</body>
</html>
*/
```

Implement Face Recognition System

```
// Sample implementation of a Face Recognition System using face-api.js
// HTML:
/*
<!DOCTYPE html>
<html>
<head>
  <script src="https://cdn.jsdelivr.net/npm/@tensorflow/tfjs"></script>
  <script src="https://cdn.jsdelivr.net/npm/@tensorflow-models/face-landmarks-
detection"></script>
  <script src="https://cdn.jsdelivr.net/npm/face-api.js"></script>
</head>
<body>
  <video id="video" width="640" height="480" autoplay></video>
  <canvas id="canvas" width="640" height="480"></canvas>
  <script>
    navigator.mediaDevices.getUserMedia({ video: true })
      .then(stream => {
        const video = document.getElementById('video');
        video.srcObject = stream;
        video.onloadedmetadata = () => {
          video.play();
          const canvas = document.getElementById('canvas');
```

```
        const context = canvas.getContext('2d');
        faceapi.nets.tinyFaceDetector.loadFromUri('/models')
          .then(() => {
            setInterval(() => {
              detectFace(video, context);
            }, 100);
          });
      };
    });

    function detectFace(video, context) {
      faceapi.detectSingleFace(video).withFaceLandmarks()
        .then(result => {
          if (result) {
            const box = result.detection.box;
            const landmarks = result.landmarks;
            // Implement face recognition logic here
            console.log('Face detected:', box);
          }
        });
    }
  </script>
</body>
</html>
*/
```

Implement Emotion Detection System

```
// Sample implementation of an Emotion Detection System using TensorFlow.js
// HTML:
/*
<!DOCTYPE html>
```

```
<html>
<head>
  <script src="https://cdn.jsdelivr.net/npm/@tensorflow/tfjs"></script>
  <script src="https://cdn.jsdelivr.net/npm/@tensorflow-models/face-expression-
recognition"></script>
</head>
<body>
  <video id="video" width="640" height="480" autoplay></video>
  <script>
    navigator.mediaDevices.getUserMedia({ video: true })
      .then(stream => {
        const video = document.getElementById('video');
        video.srcObject = stream;
        video.onloadedmetadata = () => {
          video.play();
          const model = faceExpressionRecognition.load();
          setInterval(() => {
            detectEmotion(video, model);
          }, 100);
        };
      });

    async function detectEmotion(video, model) {
      const predictions = await model.estimateFaces(video);
      if (predictions.length > 0) {
        const emotions = predictions[0].expressions;
        // Implement emotion detection logic here
        console.log('Emotions detected:', emotions);
      }
    }
  </script>
```

```
</body>
</html>
*/
```

Implement Voice-Controlled Applications

```
// Sample implementation of a Voice-Controlled Application using Web Speech API
const recognition = new webkitSpeechRecognition();
recognition.continuous = true;
recognition.lang = 'en-US';
recognition.onresult = event => {
  const transcript = event.results[event.results.length - 1][0].transcript;
  console.log('Recognized speech:', transcript);
  // Implement voice-controlled application logic here
};
recognition.start();
```

Implement Geolocation-based Services

```
// Sample implementation of Geolocation-based Services using JavaScript
if ('geolocation' in navigator) {
  navigator.geolocation.getCurrentPosition(position => {
    const latitude = position.coords.latitude;
    const longitude = position.coords.longitude;
    console.log('Current Location:', { latitude, longitude });
    // Implement geolocation-based services logic here
  }, error => {
    console.error('Error getting geolocation:', error);
  });
} else {
  console.log('Geolocation is not supported by this browser');
}
```

Implement Health Monitoring System

```
// Sample implementation of a Health Monitoring System using JavaScript
class HealthMonitoringSystem {
  constructor() {
    this.healthData = {};
  }

  addHealthData(user, heartRate, bloodPressure, temperature) {
    this.healthData[user] = { heartRate, bloodPressure, temperature };
    console.log(`Health data added for ${user}`);
  }

  displayHealthData(user) {
    console.log('Health Data:', this.healthData[user]);
  }
}

// Example usage of Health Monitoring System
const healthMonitor = new HealthMonitoringSystem();
healthMonitor.addHealthData('JohnDoe', 70, '120/80', 98.6);
healthMonitor.displayHealthData('JohnDoe');
```

Implement Emergency Response System

```
// Sample implementation of an Emergency Response System using JavaScript
class EmergencyResponseSystem {
  constructor() {
    this.emergencyContacts = [];
  }

  addEmergencyContact(name, phoneNumber) {
    this.emergencyContacts.push({ name, phoneNumber });
```

```
    console.log(`Emergency contact added: ${name} - Phone: ${phoneNumber}`);
  }

  notifyEmergencyContacts(message) {
    console.log('Emergency notification sent to contacts:');
    this.emergencyContacts.forEach(contact => {
      console.log(`- ${contact.name}: ${message}`);
    });
  }
}

// Example usage of Emergency Response System
const emergencySystem = new EmergencyResponseSystem();
emergencySystem.addEmergencyContact('John Doe', '123-456-7890');
emergencySystem.addEmergencyContact('Jane Doe', '987-654-3210');
emergencySystem.notifyEmergencyContacts('Emergency alert: Fire reported in
building.');
```

Implement Environmental Monitoring System

```
// Sample implementation of an Environmental Monitoring System using JavaScript
class EnvironmentalMonitoringSystem {
  constructor() {
    this.sensorData = {};
  }

  recordSensorData(sensorName, measurement) {
    this.sensorData[sensorName] = measurement;
    console.log(`Sensor data recorded - ${sensorName}: ${measurement}`);
  }

  analyzeSensorData() {
```

```
    console.log('Analyzing sensor data...');
    // Implement environmental data analysis logic here
  }
}

// Example usage of Environmental Monitoring System
const environmentalSystem = new EnvironmentalMonitoringSystem();
environmentalSystem.recordSensorData('Temperature', '25°C');
environmentalSystem.recordSensorData('Humidity', '50%');
environmentalSystem.analyzeSensorData();
```

Implement Smart Farming System

```
// Sample implementation of a Smart Farming System using JavaScript
class SmartFarmingSystem {
  constructor() {
    this.crops = [];
  }

  addCrop(cropName, soilMoisture, temperature) {
    this.crops.push({ cropName, soilMoisture, temperature });
    console.log(`Crop added: ${cropName} - Moisture: ${soilMoisture}, Temperature:
${temperature}`);
  }

  automateIrrigation() {
    console.log('Automating irrigation...');
    // Implement smart irrigation logic here
  }
}

// Example usage of Smart Farming System
```

```
const smartFarming = new SmartFarmingSystem();
smartFarming.addCrop('Tomatoes', 'Optimal', '25°C');
smartFarming.addCrop('Corn', 'Dry', '30°C');
smartFarming.automateIrrigation();
```

Implement Smart City Solutions

```
// Sample implementation of Smart City Solutions using JavaScript
class SmartCitySolutions {
 constructor() {
  this.services = {};
 }

 addService(serviceName, status) {
  this.services[serviceName] = status;
  console.log(`Service added: ${serviceName} - Status: ${status}`);
 }

 optimizeTraffic() {
  console.log('Optimizing traffic flow...');
  // Implement traffic management logic here
 }
}

// Example usage of Smart City Solutions
const smartCity = new SmartCitySolutions();
smartCity.addService('Public Transportation', 'Active');
smartCity.addService('Waste Management', 'Inactive');
smartCity.optimizeTraffic();
```

Implement Predictive Analytics System

```
// Sample implementation of a Predictive Analytics System using TensorFlow.js
// Example: Training a Linear Regression model
const tf = require('@tensorflow/tfjs');

const xs = tf.tensor2d([[1], [2], [3], [4]], [4, 1]);
const ys = tf.tensor2d([[2], [4], [6], [8]], [4, 1]);

const model = tf.sequential();
model.add(tf.layers.dense({ units: 1, inputShape: [1] }));

model.compile({ optimizer: 'sgd', loss: 'meanSquaredError' });
model.fit(xs, ys, { epochs: 100 })
  .then(() => {
    const prediction = model.predict(tf.tensor2d([[5]], [1, 1]));
    prediction.print();
  });
```

Implement Data Mining Applications

```
// Sample implementation of a Data Mining Application using JavaScript
// Example: Apriori Algorithm for frequent itemset mining
class DataMiningApplication {
  constructor(transactions, minSupport) {
    this.transactions = transactions;
    this.minSupport = minSupport;
  }

  findFrequentItemsets() {
    // Implement Apriori algorithm or other data mining techniques
    console.log('Frequent itemsets found:');
    // Example output:
```

```
    console.log(['A'], ['B'], ['C']);
  }
}

// Example usage of Data Mining Application
const transactions = [
  ['A', 'B', 'C'],
  ['A', 'C'],
  ['B', 'D'],
  ['A', 'B', 'D'],
  ['B', 'C']
];

const dataMiningApp = new DataMiningApplication(transactions, 0.4);
dataMiningApp.findFrequentItemsets();
```

Implement Blockchain Applications

```
// Sample implementation of a Blockchain Application using JavaScript
const SHA256 = require('crypto-js/sha256');

class Block {
  constructor(index, timestamp, data, previousHash = '') {
    this.index = index;
    this.timestamp = timestamp;
    this.data = data;
    this.previousHash = previousHash;
    this.hash = this.calculateHash();
  }

  calculateHash() {
```

```
    return SHA256(this.index + this.previousHash + this.timestamp +
JSON.stringify(this.data)).toString();
  }
}

class Blockchain {
  constructor() {
    this.chain = [this.createGenesisBlock()];
  }

  createGenesisBlock() {
    return new Block(0, '01/01/2024', 'Genesis Block', '0');
  }

  addBlock(newBlock) {
    newBlock.previousHash = this.chain[this.chain.length - 1].hash;
    newBlock.hash = newBlock.calculateHash();
    this.chain.push(newBlock);
  }

  isValid() {
    for (let i = 1; i < this.chain.length; i++) {
      const currentBlock = this.chain[i];
      const previousBlock = this.chain[i - 1];

      if (currentBlock.hash !== currentBlock.calculateHash() ||
          currentBlock.previousHash !== previousBlock.hash) {
        return false;
      }
    }
    return true;
```

```
  }
}

// Example usage of Blockchain
const myBlockchain = new Blockchain();
myBlockchain.addBlock(new Block(1, '01/02/2024', { amount: 10 }));
myBlockchain.addBlock(new Block(2, '01/03/2024', { amount: 20 }));
console.log('Blockchain is valid:', myBlockchain.isValid());
```

Implement Cybersecurity Tools

```
// Sample implementation of Cybersecurity Tools using JavaScript
// Example: Password hashing with bcrypt
const bcrypt = require('bcryptjs');

const password = 'MySecurePassword123';

bcrypt.hash(password, 10)
  .then(hash => {
    console.log('Hashed password:', hash);

    bcrypt.compare(password, hash)
      .then(match => {
        console.log('Password match:', match);
      })
      .catch(error => {
        console.error('Error comparing passwords:', error);
      });
  })
  .catch(error => {
    console.error('Error hashing password:', error);
  });
```

Implement Virtual Classroom

```
// Sample implementation of a Virtual Classroom using JavaScript
class VirtualClassroom {
  constructor() {
    this.students = [];
    this.currentTopic = '';
  }

  enrollStudent(studentName) {
    this.students.push(studentName);
    console.log(`Student enrolled: ${studentName}`);
  }

  startLesson(topic) {
    this.currentTopic = topic;
    console.log(`Lesson started on: ${topic}`);
  }

  displayStudents() {
    console.log('Enrolled Students:', this.students);
  }
}

// Example usage of Virtual Classroom
const virtualClassroom = new VirtualClassroom();
virtualClassroom.enrollStudent('John Doe');
virtualClassroom.enrollStudent('Jane Doe');
virtualClassroom.startLesson('JavaScript Basics');
virtualClassroom.displayStudents();
```

Implement Online Exam System

```
// Sample implementation of an Online Exam System using JavaScript
class OnlineExamSystem {
  constructor() {
    this.questions = [];
    this.answers = {};
  }

  addQuestion(question, options, correctAnswer) {
    this.questions.push({ question, options, correctAnswer });
  }

  submitAnswer(studentName, questionIndex, answer) {
    if (!this.answers[studentName]) {
      this.answers[studentName] = {};
    }
    this.answers[studentName][questionIndex] = answer;
    console.log(`Answer submitted by ${studentName} for question ${questionIndex}`);
  }

  gradeExam(studentName) {
    if (this.answers[studentName]) {
      let score = 0;
      this.questions.forEach((question, index) => {
        if (this.answers[studentName][index] === question.correctAnswer) {
          score++;
        }
      });
      console.log(`Exam graded for ${studentName}. Score:
${score}/${this.questions.length}`);
    } else {
```

```
      console.log(`No answers submitted for ${studentName}`);
    }
  }
}

// Example usage of Online Exam System
const onlineExam = new OnlineExamSystem();
onlineExam.addQuestion('What is 2 + 2?', ['2', '3', '4', '5'], '4');
onlineExam.addQuestion('Who is the president of USA?', ['Trump', 'Biden', 'Obama',
'Bush'], 'Biden');
onlineExam.submitAnswer('John Doe', 0, '4');
onlineExam.submitAnswer('John Doe', 1, 'Biden');
onlineExam.gradeExam('John Doe');
```

Implement Digital Wallet

```
// Sample implementation of a Digital Wallet using JavaScript
class DigitalWallet {
  constructor() {
    this.balance = 0;
    this.transactions = [];
  }

  deposit(amount) {
    this.balance += amount;
    this.transactions.push({ type: 'Deposit', amount });
    console.log(`Deposited: ${amount}`);
  }

  withdraw(amount) {
    if (this.balance >= amount) {
      this.balance -= amount;
```

```
      this.transactions.push({ type: 'Withdrawal', amount });
      console.log(`Withdrawn: ${amount}`);
    } else {
      console.log('Insufficient balance');
    }
  }

  displayTransactions() {
    console.log('Transaction History:', this.transactions);
  }
}

// Example usage of Digital Wallet
const wallet = new DigitalWallet();
wallet.deposit(100);
wallet.withdraw(50);
wallet.displayTransactions();
```

Implement Online Insurance System

```
// Sample implementation of an Online Insurance System using JavaScript
class OnlineInsuranceSystem {
  constructor() {
    this.policies = {};
  }

  purchasePolicy(policyHolder, policyType, premium) {
    this.policies[policyHolder] = { policyType, premium };
    console.log(`Policy purchased by ${policyHolder}: ${policyType} - Premium:
${premium}`);
  }
```

```
  cancelPolicy(policyHolder) {
    if (this.policies[policyHolder]) {
      delete this.policies[policyHolder];
      console.log(`Policy cancelled for ${policyHolder}`);
    } else {
      console.log(`Policy not found for ${policyHolder}`);
    }
  }
  displayPolicies() {
    console.log('Active Policies:', this.policies);
  }
}

// Example usage of Online Insurance System
const insuranceSystem = new OnlineInsuranceSystem();
insuranceSystem.purchasePolicy('John Doe', 'Health Insurance', '$100/month');
insuranceSystem.purchasePolicy('Jane Doe', 'Car Insurance', '$500/year');
insuranceSystem.displayPolicies();
insuranceSystem.cancelPolicy('John Doe');
insuranceSystem.displayPolicies();
```

Implement E-voting System

```
// Sample implementation of an E-voting System using JavaScript
class EVotingSystem {
  constructor() {
    this.candidates = {};
    this.votes = {};
  }

  addCandidate(candidateName) {
    this.candidates[candidateName] = 0;
```

```
    console.log(`Candidate added: ${candidateName}`);
  }

  voteForCandidate(candidateName) {
    if (this.candidates[candidateName] !== undefined) {
      this.candidates[candidateName]++;
      console.log(`Vote recorded for ${candidateName}`);
    } else {
      console.log(`Candidate ${candidateName} not found`);
    }
  }

  tallyVotes() {
    console.log('Election Results:');
    Object.entries(this.candidates).forEach(([candidate, votes]) => {
      console.log(`${candidate}: ${votes} votes`);
    });
  }
}
// Example usage of E-voting System
const eVotingSystem = new EVotingSystem();
eVotingSystem.addCandidate('Candidate A');
eVotingSystem.addCandidate('Candidate B');
eVotingSystem.voteForCandidate('Candidate A');
eVotingSystem.voteForCandidate('Candidate B');
eVotingSystem.voteForCandidate('Candidate A');
eVotingSystem.tallyVotes();
```

www.ingramcontent.com/pod-product-compliance
Lightning Source LLC
LaVergne TN
LVHW010559160826
845677LV00013B/3182

* 9 7 8 9 3 3 4 0 5 7 8 6 7 *